What a book to be written in an era when people are suppressing the truth only because they do not want to believe the gospel! The book simplifies and summarizes the complexity of sixty-six books of the Bible. It helps the reader to understand the unity and one true story of God's plan to save mankind as it unfolds in the Bible. It removes doubt about issues in the Bible which seem not to be clear to many. Indeed it is a gospel—good news—presentation.

—Amos Magezi, director of the Uganda Bible Institute, Mbarara, Uganda

What an ideal book for a generation which is biblically illiterate, yet fascinated by stories! For Iain Campbell shows how the Bible tells the greatest of all stories—which has moreover the merit of being true. Taken together, these seven highlights of God's saving activity provide a rounded picture of the Person in whom alone salvation is to be found—the Lord Jesus Christ. Dr Campbell has mastered the art of profound simplicity, with a wealth of teaching contained in an accessible and fascinating narrative. 'Wonderful' in more than one sense!

—Edward Donnelly, Minister, Trinity Reformed Presbyterian Church, Newtownabbey and Principal, Reformed Theological College, Belfast

W0007835

Introduction

My purpose in this little book is to present the gospel, the 'good news' message of salvation, which focuses on the Lord Jesus Christ. That message is told us in the Bible, and this book is a retelling of the story. I'd like to thank Day One Publications for their willingness to help me tell it.

Our world does not like absolute truth, or propositional statements. It is profoundly suspicious of religious texts; yet the Bible is the source for the story of God's salvation. The drama of redemption is rooted and grounded in the God who acted, and who continues to act in human history that his glory might be displayed and enjoyed by us.

I've focused here on seven pivotal points of salvation history—what I've called the seven wonders of the world. Read the story, then read the epilogue, and put your trust in Jesus Christ.

Iain D Campbell

Contents

1 THE WONDER OF CREATION   **6**

2 THE WONDER OF REDEMPTION   **16**

3 THE WONDER OF INHERITANCE   **29**

4 THE WONDER OF INCARNATION   **45**

5 THE WONDER OF RESURRECTION   **57**

6 THE WONDER OF PENTECOST   **68**

7 THE WONDER OF CHRIST'S GLORIOUS APPEARING   **82**

EPILOGUE: WHAT NOW?   **90**

The wonder of creation

In the beginning God created the heavens and the earth (Genesis 1:1).

S o begins the Bible—and the story of the world has its origins in this tremendous moment, in which God began to create all things out of nothing. Some modern-day readers of the Bible regard Genesis as a myth—but not one of the biblical authors adopts that position. Consider the following testimonies throughout Scripture:

Hezekiah says, 'O LORD, the God of Israel, enthroned above the cherubim, you are the God, you alone, of all the kingdoms of the earth; *you have made heaven and earth*' (2 Kings 19:15).

David says, 'All the gods of the peoples are idols, but *the LORD made the heavens*' (1 Chronicles 16:26).

Nehemiah says, 'You are the LORD, you alone. *You have made heaven*, the heaven of heavens, with all their host, the earth and all that is on it, the seas and all that is in them; and you preserve all of them; and the host of heaven worships you' (Nehemiah 9:6).

Solomon says, 'As you do not know the way the spirit comes to the bones in the womb of a woman with child, so you do not know the work of *God who makes everything*' (Ecclesiastes 11:5).

Isaiah says, 'Thus says *God, the LORD, who created the heavens* and stretched them out, who spread out the earth and what comes from it, who gives breath to the people on it and spirit to those who walk in it: "I am the LORD"' (Isaiah 42:5–6).

Amos says, 'For behold, *he who forms the mountains and creates the wind*, and declares to man what is his thought, who makes the morning darkness, and treads on the heights of the earth—the LORD, the God of hosts, is his name!' (Amos 4:13).

John says, '*All things were made through him*, and without him was not any thing made that was made' (John 1:3).

Paul says, 'To me, though I am the very least of all the saints, this grace was given, to preach to the Gentiles the unsearchable riches of Christ, and to bring to light for everyone what is the plan of the mystery hidden for ages in *God who created all things*' (Ephesians 3:8–9).

And in the Book of Revelation, an angel raises his hand and swears, 'by him who lives for ever and ever, *who created heaven and what is in it, the earth and what is in it*' (Revelation 10:6).

The testimony of Scripture is that the world in which we live, together with everything that makes up the vast universe—every star and moon, every planet and galaxy, every species of animal and bird, every human life—owes its origin to God. If the Bible teaches anything, it teaches that God is our Creator. Every subsequent chapter of Bible history, as well as every chapter of secular history, is grounded in the truth of Genesis chapter 1, and the doctrine that 'God did in the beginning, by the word of his power, make of nothing the world, and all things therein, for himself, within the space of six days, and all very good' (*Westminster Larger Catechism*, Q.15).

The importance of creation

Moses, the author of Genesis, clearly had a purpose in writing Genesis 1. Perhaps the purpose was to show the glory of the God of Israel over against the powerlessness and impotency of the idols of other nations. His purpose was *polemical,* 'to repudiate the polytheistic cosmology of his day; to insist that the entire universe was the creation of the one, living God of Israel; and to proclaim that every other pretended deity was a creature, and a vassal of this God. This is why there is such explicit stress on the creation of the sun, the moon and the stars, so often objects of worship in the ancient world'.[1]

Another purpose of Genesis 1, however, is to lead us to a sense of *wonder,* as we see that 'the heavens declare the glory of God, and the sky above proclaims his handiwork' (Psalm 19:1); to lead us to say 'I will praise you, for I am fearfully and wonderfully made. Wonderful are your works; my soul knows it very well' (Psalm 139:14); to lead us at last to sing with the choirs of heaven, 'Worthy are you, our Lord and God, to receive glory and honour and power, for you created all things, and by your will they existed and were created' (Revelation 4:11).

And that is one of the reasons why the doctrine of creation is so important to us today. We must move beyond our wonder at the creation to our wonder at the Creator: beyond every sunset and every breathtaking view, beyond every snow-capped mountain and every winding river, beyond the artistry of the composition—changing landscapes, colourful seasons, varying climates—to the glory of the artist, which is revealed and displayed at every point.

That's where the story begins, in Genesis 1, with the creation of the universe. So what does Genesis 1 give us? I suggest there are four things:

A personal God

The story of the creation of all things begins, not with the world, but with God. 'In the beginning, God created.' We must have either a *theistic* (God-centred) or an *atheistic* (God-denying) view of how everything began. There is no other option. What existed before the world existed? Either God did, or nothing did. If you take God out of your answer to that question, you need to put something else in his place—but what else can provide the answers to the fundamental question of our origin? Either everything came from nothing or everything came from something. The Christian world view believes that everything came from someone, and that someone is God. The way we approach this issue will colour the whole of our lives.

Douglas Kelly has written,

Tragedy and despair—in both ancient and modern forms—are based on a view that there is not a creation nor a Creator but that at the back of everything are impersonal forces, so that the Universe is faceless: it is ultimately dark out there. Such emptiness makes a tremendous difference in how to view everyday life as well as how to handle the mysteries of existence.[2]

The added wonder of the biblical doctrine is that behind the face of the creation is the face of God, and we can see it in Jesus Christ. It is from him and through him and to him, in him, by him and for him, that all things are made (Romans 11:36). 'Creation is Christ-shaped.'[3] So with Hebrews 11:3 we say, 'By faith we understand that the universe was created by the word of God, so that what is seen was not made out of things that are visible.'

There is a God, independent of the world, self-existent, omnipotent—that is, almighty. He is the sovereign, and it is in him that we live and move and have our being (Acts 17:28). The wonder is that he is still engaged with his world, and has not left it at the mercy of created forces. His mind created matter; matter did not create our minds.

The problem is, as Paul reminds us in Romans 1, that we have distorted our view of God through our sin. Instead of worshipping and glorifying and resting in this God, we have worshipped created things instead of the Creator (Romans 1:25). Sin has upset the equilibrium. This is not how things should be.

Yet is it true of us that we are living for *things*—temporal, created things—that are ready to pass away and perish with the using? Our focus is to be on eternal realities (2 Corinthians 4:18), and on the One who made all things.

A powerful word

The second element of Genesis 1 is the fact of God's word. God *spoke* the world into existence. Before God spoke, there was nothing. After God spoke, there was something. But the something could not just come out of nothing. Nor is the something eternal. The world is not eternal. Matter is not eternal. It has a point of origin, because

By the word of the LORD the heavens were made,
and by qthe breath of his mouth all rtheir host.
He gathers the waters of the sea as sa heap;
he tputs the deeps in storehouses. (Psalm 33:6–7).

Let's be clear on this: the world was made *by God,* not *out of God.* It reflects God's glory, but is not to be identified with the God whose glory it declares. We must be clear on this point. It is our Heavenly Father we worship, not Mother Earth.

But he said 'Let there be light', and there was light. This is 'God's lordship attribute *of authority*'.4 It is the power of his word to create that is brought before us in Genesis 1. This means at least three things.

His word *originates* his creation. There might not have been a creation.

But there is: and it is his speaking that brings it into being. God's direct speech 'drives and forms the account'.[5] It alone is able to enter the nothingness and bring something out. And it is the resultant creation that shows what has been in God's mind; his creative word reveals his creative thought, intention and purpose.

His word *conserves* his creation. The events of day two do not negate the events of day one; there is light on day two just as it was created on day one. 'God is not only the *originating* cause of the universe, but he is also its *conserving* cause. He caused it to come to be, and he also causes it to continue to be … creation is contingent at all times—it is always dependent on its Creator. Once a creature, always a creature'.[6] As his word causes the world to be, so it causes it to continue to be: it *becomes* the world through his word, and it continues to *be* the world through his word.

His word *interprets* his creation. He names the *day* and the *night*, and 'established a linguistic system in which the true nature of everything could be expressed'.[7] We are able to define things because we are in the image of the Creator. The Genesis narrative not only announces God as solo artist, but also tells us his verdict: 'he saw that it was all very good.' This evaluation is part of the interpretation.

It is this same word which, according to Paul, can bring new life into our souls. 'For God, who said, "Let light shine out of darkness", has shone in our hearts to give the light of the knowledge of the glory of God in the face of Jesus Christ' (2 Corinthians 4:6). He alone can bring a new creation out of an old one, just as he brought the first creation out of nothing.

A progressive creation

The third element is the fact of progress in God's action. The work of creation takes place over six days. A debate has raged over the meaning of the word 'day' in Genesis 1. There are those who believe that these six days were, literally, 24–hour periods; there are others that argue from the fact that sometimes the Bible can use the word 'day' in a non-literal sense (for example, in the phrase, 'Abraham saw my day' in John 8:56). The theologian Charles Hodge took the view that if the natural sense of the passage is inconsistent with other facts, then we need to take a view other than the natural one. In this way he could argue that these creation days were long periods, and thus harmonize them with scientific theory. At the same time, Hodge reacted violently to the evolutionary theories of Charles Darwin and his followers, because they presented a creation with no purpose or meaning at all.

I do believe, however, not only that the Hebrew forms used in Genesis 1 make the literal 'day' the more natural reading of the passage, but that we must understand it in this way. In Genesis 1:5, for example, what we read in the original Hebrew is not 'and there was evening and there was morning, the first day' (an ordinal number), but 'there was evening and there was morning, one day' (a cardinal number). In other words, God defines what a day is: a period of light, divided from darkness. It was not necessary for the sun to be created in order to define the length of a day; that is established at the beginning. Every other day follows this pattern.

It is also important to note the absence of the definite article 'the': it is *one day*, not *the* first day. In fact, the definite article does not appear until *the sixth day*, which is a climactic day. So the usage of the Hebrew language in verse 5 sets the pattern, a pattern which is corroborated by the appearance of lights to govern the days God had made. Time is created as well as the material creation.

So, as Bruce Waltke puts it,

Utilizing the structure of the creative process, the narrator constructs the story with billowing detail and movement. With crescendo the narrator devotes more time and space to each day until the climactic apex of creation, when motion ceases, and God rests.[8]

The first three days and the second three days balance each other. In the first three days, God creates the resources which give form and shape to the universe: Day 1, the light; Day 2, the sky and seas; Day 3, the dry land and vegetation. In the second three days, he creates what will fill and use these resources: Day 4, the sun, moon and stars; Day 5, the birds and fish; Day 6, animals and man. Now the universe is no longer 'without form and void': it has a shape, and it is filled.

And at the apex of creation is God's crowning act of sovereign lordship: the creation of man. This aspect is a fundamentally important element of the creation story. Our origins are important. We need to know *how* we were made, and *why* we were made. Atheistic science puts it all down to the throw of the cosmic dice, and talks of natural selection. But there, too, the folly is exposed: how can nature select? Even with the removal of God, something personal is required to fill the void.

The tragedy of our modern age is that the removal of God has had profound consequences for anthropology. Take away the glory of God and you take away the dignity of man. Both are intimately connected and intertwined. With the increasing secularization of our culture we have witnessed the most horrendous growth in abortions, coupled with the legalization of euthanasia in some parts of the world. Only the recovery of a sense of God can help us recapture the sense of man's value and dignity.

So, what makes man different?

First, before God makes man, he takes counsel and makes a deliberate decision to do so (Genesis 1:26). Man is the focus of God's special care and attention, not made on a whim, but after careful, deliberate and purposeful counsel. Suddenly, after the repetition of verbs in which one being acts, there is now consultation, collaboration and counsel, in which a plurality of agents is introduced. It is not 'let there be' but 'let us make'. In actual fact, the plurality has been present in the Hebrew text, where the word for 'God' is 'elohim', a plural form. Evangelical biblical scholars have seen here the roots of the New Testament doctrine of the Trinity. God is one God; yet there is a personal plurality within that Godhead.

Second, man is artistically made. In Genesis 1:26, the creating verb is simply the word 'make'. But in Genesis 2:7 we read that *God formed* man from the dust of the ground. The word that is used there is the word used in Jeremiah 18 of the work of the potter as he shapes and fashions his jars and vases out of the clay. There is the implication of design, of care, of patterning, of watchfulness. Man emerges from God's creative hand as the most magnificent of all his works.

Third, God also imposes a blueprint: man is to be created 'after God's image'. Man is unique in God's creation. He is the most Creator-like creature there is. There are aspects of personality, construction and design which God finds in himself and transfers into what he models out of the soil. The highest possible concepts are used when God makes man. Man does not evolve out of the animal kingdom. He is not simply the product of development from lower forms of life. He was always intended to be the highest.

Clearly the 'image' referred to here includes both body and soul. John Calvin makes the interesting suggestion at one point that whereas animals were created to walk on four legs and look downwards to the earth, man was made upright, with the ability to look upwards to the heavens. That is an intriguing thought, which at least serves to remind us that when God made man's body out of the dust, he made it in a way that was congruous not only with the nature of his environment, but also with the nature of his God.

The image also includes human sexuality: God made man male and female. The Hebrew literally says that he 'built' woman, because he took Adam's rib and fashioned it into a human body with female characteristics. The woman, therefore, has characteristics which relate her to her environment, to her Maker *and* to her husband. This, of course, has tremendous implications for our sexual morals and ethics, both for marriage and divorce (see Matthew 19:4ff) and for homosexuality, which the Bible declares to be sinful (Romans 1:26ff).

Finally, being made in God's image means that humans alone, of all creation, can communicate with their Maker. Birds and fish and animals don't pray. They give glory to the Creator in different ways, but they do not assemble to praise him, or live in his presence. Man can. 'Being made in God's image establishes humanity's role on earth and facilitates communication with the divine.'9 Man can talk to the animals; but more importantly, he can talk to their Maker.

And the implication of the passage, too, is that man will be able to relate to God as Trinity. He will relate to the Father. He will relate to the Son. He will relate to the Holy Spirit. The mystery—one of our seven 'wonders'—is that one of these divine Persons will relate to man in a remarkable way, when he takes on himself our nature, with all its infirmities and weaknesses. But the point of the creation account is simple: man is made to know God in all the fullness of his divine being.

Fourth, God does not make man *immediately*, but *mediately*, out of the dust of the ground. The highest plan is imposed on the least element of earth. God shapes a body for him, then breathes life into him. Man is everything, yet he is nothing. When sin robs man of his dignity, distorts the image of God in him, and severs body and soul, he will return to his constituent element. Yet he still remains wonderfully made.

Then, ultimately, there is the Sabbath rest, setting a pattern which is incorporated in the fourth commandment: 'Remember the Sabbath day, to keep it holy. Six days you shall labour, and do all your work ... for in six days the LORD made heaven and earth, the sea, and all that is in them, and rested on the seventh day. Therefore the LORD blessed the Sabbath day and made it holy' (Exodus 20:8–11). 'In the first six days, space is subdued; on the seventh, time is sanctified.'[10]

In spite of the fact that many evangelical Christians argue that there is no New Testament warrant for the ongoing authority of the fourth commandment, there is an important principle here which is older than Sinai and which goes right back to creation. The blueprint for a day of rest is set before us in the example of God himself, of whom four things were true on day seven of creation week: he *ended* his work, he *rested* from it, he *blessed* the day, and he *sanctified* it. And, as Jesus reminds us, he did this for man (Mark 2:27), for the benefit of mankind and the world. Jesus also declares that he, as the Son of Man, is lord of the sabbath (Mark 2:28). If the Sabbath principle is no longer valid in the New Testament, therefore, of what is the Son of Man lord?

Theologians often speak of the *creation ordinances* of labour, marriage and the Sabbath. These were built into the fabric and cycle of the world God made. Adam and Eve were to work to the glory of God, they were to be faithful to each other in marriage, and they were to observe the Sabbath rest as a day of worship to God. This means that even if the world had continued as God made it, without the entrance of sin, without death, without rebellion—had there continued to be a perfect society for man to dwell in, then the three things which would have remained necessary for that society to function would be work, marriage and the Sabbath. Lose any of these, and you are on the road to society's disintegration.

There is, however, something else in all of this.

A purposeful world

What can we say about the reason why God did this wonderful thing? Why did he make the world?

In the highest sense, God made the world for his own glory. He made it so that it would, indeed, declare the glory of God. And because that is so, our highest good and our 'chief end' is 'to glorify God and to enjoy him for ever'. Only biblical creation can supply us with this reason for living. If evolution is true, and we originated in some other way, we have nothing to do, but to 'eat, drink and be merry'. But if the Bible is true, then our purpose for living is the same as God's purpose in creating: to give all the glory to him.

And that glory is seen in the fact that God's world becomes the theatre of history. And when sin mars it, it will be the stage on which the drama of redemption will be enacted. Finally, God will remake it in some form which will recapture its original purpose and glory: 'according to his promise, we are waiting for new heavens and a new earth in which righteousness dwells' (2 Peter 3:13).

Oh come, let us worship and bow down;
let us kneel before the LORD, our Maker!
For he is our God,
and we are the people of his pasture,
and the sheep of his hand (Psalm 95:6–7).

Notes

1 **Donald Macleod,** *A Faith to Live by* (Fearn, Tain: Mentor, 1999), p. 60.

2 **Douglas F. Kelly,** *Creation and Change* (Fearn, Tain: Mentor, 1997), p. 29.

3 **Macleod,** p. 64.

4 **John Frame,** *The Doctrine of God* (Phillipsburg, NJ: Presbyterian and Reformed, 2002), p. 293.

5 **Bruce K. Waltke,** *Genesis: A Commentary* (Grand Rapids, MI: Zondervan, 2001), p. 56.

6 **Norman Geisler,** *Systematic Theology,* Vol. 2 (Minneapolis, MN: Bethany House, 2002–2005), p. 444.

7 **Frame,** p. 294.

8 **Waltke,** *Genesis,* p. 57.

9 Ibid. p. 65.

10 Ibid. p. 67.

The wonder of redemption

At the end of 430 years, on that very day, all the hosts of the LORD went out from the land of Egypt (Exodus 12:41).

Having looked at the wonder of creation, we come now to the second of the seven wonders of the Bible, the second pivotal point on which the Bible's story hangs. Before coming to it, we'll rehearse the events that took place following the creation of the world.

Although created in perfection, Adam and Eve sinned against God. Their rebellion was not merely some personal act of transgression—it was an action in which the whole of mankind was implicated. Adam was not merely an individual—he was also a public, representative person, in whom we all sinned when he fell. The fellowship between him and God was ruptured, and Paradise was lost to him. But God did not leave him without hope; in Genesis 3:15 God promised that the seed of the woman would crush the serpent's head; one day, God himself would provide the answer to man's sin.

So Genesis, as it continues to tell the primitive history of mankind, also tells a twofold story: the story of the consequences of sin, and the story of the revelation of grace. Sin is seen in what takes place between Adam's sons, Cain and Abel. Cain kills Abel, and experiences God's curse. It is the beginning of enmity and hatred between those who love God, as Abel did, and those who do not. God gives Adam and Eve another son, Seth, through whose descendants God will preserve his church.

The wickedness of the world peaks to such a degree that God can tolerate it no longer, so in Genesis 6 we read about God's judgement by way of a flood. The story of God's grace is seen in the provision of an ark by which Noah and his family are saved, on top of which God reiterates his covenant promise in Genesis 9. He will not again destroy the earth with a flood; instead, he will bless the line of Shem, Noah's son, with the blessing of his salvation. Thus intimation is given that the Semitic (derived from Shem's name) line of the Jews will carry the story of God's grace until the promised deliverer comes.

The story of sin again peaks in the attempt to build a tower to reach heaven (Genesis 11); the story of grace continues in the history of Abraham. The covenant promise is renewed in Genesis 12—through Abraham the world is to be blessed. He and his seed will have a special place in God's purpose, and in spite of personal failings on their part, grace will preserve God's honour and God's people. God continues to work in the family of Isaac, Abraham's son, then in the family of Jacob, with whom God confirms his saving plan, and to whom he gives the name Israel.

Much of the second part of Genesis focuses on Jacob and his sons, particularly in the way Joseph is forcibly taken to Egypt, where, through the evil scheming of his master's wife, he is imprisoned. But God is with him, and he rises to become Pharaoh's prime minister. Through his wise leadership at a time of famine, many are preserved, not least the sons of Jacob who engineered Joseph's being sold as a slave, simply because they were jealous of him.

One of the results is that Jacob's sons reside in Egypt, and their descendants remain there for over four centuries. But times change. Joseph is forgotten. Pharaoh becomes suspicious of the growing number of the sons of Israel, and, in order to prevent them rising up and rebelling against the Egyptians, he makes them his slaves. That is the point at which Exodus opens.

The importance of the book of Exodus
This second book of the Bible continues what Genesis has told us about the twin themes of sin and grace. But in addition, it adds substantially to it. The Book of Exodus is important for at least three reasons.

FIRST, THE BOOK OF EXODUS INTRODUCES US TO THE UNIQUE CHARACTER OF MOSES
Moses is a descendant of Jacob, and is miraculously saved from death at birth. In order to keep down the number of Israelites, Pharaoh decrees that male children are to be thrown into the River Nile at birth. But Moses' mother will not do such a thing, and Moses is not only saved from death but raised by none other than the daughter of Pharaoh herself. After many years in exile in Midian, God reveals himself to Moses in Horeb (Exodus

3), commissioning him to go to Pharaoh and to secure the release of his people. It is a task which Moses will carry out diligently—a later writer will say of him that 'Moses was faithful in all God's house' (Hebrews 3:2).

But it is not simply as a redeemer that Moses is to occupy a unique position in God's purpose. He is also a prophet, with whom God communicates in a remarkable way. God reveals his law to Moses; he reveals the nature of worship to Moses; he reveals his purposes and intentions to Moses. Through Moses, a record of this ancient history is preserved for us in the Pentateuch, the first five books of the Bible. And ultimately, the conclusion of the Scriptures is that 'there has not arisen a prophet since in Israel like Moses, whom the LORD knew face to face, none like him for all the signs and the wonders that the LORD sent him to do in the land of Egypt, to Pharaoh and to all his servants and to all his land, and for all the mighty power and all the great deeds of terror that Moses did in the sight of all Israel' (Deuteronomy 34:10–12).

Not until Jesus appeared did anyone approximate to Moses' degree of closeness to God and status before God. And when Jesus, the last prophet, came, he surpassed Moses in the way a son surpasses a servant (Hebrews 3:5–6). But Moses' life, and the way the life is told to us in the Book of Exodus, parallels that of Christ to such a degree that we can say that he is a 'type' or 'prefigurement' of Jesus. Moses was a symbol to the Israelites of the personification of God's purpose of grace; now God's grace is revealed personally to us with the coming of God himself in the Person of Jesus Christ.

SECOND, THE BOOK OF EXODUS HELPS TO IDENTIFY GOD'S PEOPLE
Throughout the Old Testament, God's people are going to be characterized by the events that take place at this point of history. Consider the following verses:

Deuteronomy 21:8: 'Accept atonement, O LORD, for your people Israel, *whom you have redeemed ...*'

1 Chronicles 17:21: 'Who is like your people Israel, the one nation on earth *whom God went to redeem* to be his people, making for yourself a name for great and awesome things, in driving out nations before your people whom you redeemed from Egypt?'

Nehemiah 1:10: 'They are your servants and your people, *whom you have redeemed* by your great power and by your strong hand.'

Psalm 77:15: 'You with your arm *redeemed your people,* the children of Jacob and Joseph.'

Psalm 107:2: 'Let *the redeemed of the* LORD say so, whom he has redeemed from trouble …'

Isaiah 52:9: 'Break forth together into singing, you waste places of Jerusalem, for the LORD has comforted his people; *he has redeemed Jerusalem.'*

Jeremiah 31:11: 'For the LORD has ransomed Jacob *and has redeemed him* from hands too strong for him.'

Zechariah 10:8: 'I will whistle for them and gather them in, for *I have redeemed them,* and they shall be as many as they were before.'

Galatians 3:13: '*Christ redeemed us* from the curse of the law by becoming a curse for us.'

The subsequent history of the Old Testament shows that God's people will forever be characterized by the fact of their redemption. They are not known for their numerical strength, or their earthly glory, but simply as the people God redeemed. For that reason, he will not let them down. For that reason, they must serve him. For that reason, they are forever joined to him in a covenant bond that nothing must sever. So the redemption of which our chapter speaks is going to be the greatest, chief characteristic of God's people from this point of time onwards.

This challenges the myth that we are all God's children. Yes, there is a sense in which the prophet Malachi can ask, 'Have we not all one Father? Has not one God created us?' (Malachi 2:10); but we have also all rebelled against our Father. We need to be redeemed. Early on in the Bible we are reminded that God's people are those whom he has saved from their sins, whom he has redeemed. This is summarized for us by Paul in Colossians

1:13–4: 'He has delivered us from the domain of darkness and transferred us to the kingdom of his beloved Son, in whom we have redemption, the forgiveness of sins.'

THIRD, THE BOOK OF EXODUS TEACHES US THE VOCABULARY OF THE GOSPEL
The language of the gospel is the language of redemption, to which we are introduced in the Book of Exodus. For example, Exodus 12 emphasizes the role of a lamb; John points to Jesus and says 'Behold, the Lamb of God' (John 1:29). It emphasizes the role of blood; the New Testament frequently refers to our salvation by the blood of Christ (Romans 5:9, Hebrews 9:14). It talks of passover; Christ is explicitly said to be our passover (1 Corinthians 5:7). It refers to unleavened bread, a concept which is used by both Jesus and the apostles (Mark 8:15; 1 Corinthians 5:8). It refers to the Passover feast, specifically designed to commemorate the redemptive work of God, which is of significance for the New Testament Lord's Supper (Matthew 26:26–29).

Without the Old Testament story, we cannot understand the New Testament gospel. The language in which the good news is expressed is rooted in these events here. God made a way out for his people: that is what the word 'exodus' means. And it is interesting that in the Transfiguration incident in the New Testament, where Moses and Elijah speak with Jesus, it is of his 'exodus' that they speak (Luke 9:31). His work as redeemer is to secure redemption. The roots of that redemptive activity are here in God's determination to save his people out of Egypt.

So how is the wonder of God's redemptive work seen in this book? Let's think of several issues.

The need for redemption—slavery

God's people require to be redeemed, for two specific reasons:

First, they are in bondage. They are slaves in a land where they ought to be free. They groan under their taskmasters where once they enjoyed property and provision. God's redemptive work will address that need and will secure their freedom. To 'redeem' literally means to 'buy back' (from its Latin root), although the Greek word for redemption really has at its core the idea of 'loosing'. Thus what God does in Egypt tells us as much about sin as it does about grace. It reminds us that sin binds; it acts in tyrannical, despotic fashion, keeping us in bondage until we are liberated. What Adam and Eve thought would free them to greater enjoyment actually binds them to deeper misery.

The language Paul uses about sin in Romans 6 is precisely the same. 'Do you not know that if you present yourselves to anyone as obedient slaves, you are slaves of the one whom you obey, either of sin, which leads to death, or of obedience, which leads to righteousness?' (Romans 6:16). There is no liberty to be enjoyed in the path of disobedience; sin only leads to slavery, bondage and entrapment.

And the second reason why redemption is necessary is precisely because God's people cannot free themselves. The slavery is complete and includes inability. They are powerless to make themselves free. Everything about them is hedged around by the limitations of their captivity, and a change of status is impossible without God's help. Apart from his intervention, the state of bondage will remain. But with his intervention, there can be the prospect and the hope of a change of condition.

This is precisely the terminology of the gospel. Leave a person alone and he or she will die in sin. Without grace a person dies a captive, with every fibre of that person's being dominated by sin's power and might. But bring in the amazing grace of God and chains can be loosed, the prison can be unlocked, and the captive can go free. Jesus, our Redeemer, our Lamb, our Passover, was very conscious of the fact that this was precisely the nature of his mission, as he declares to us that 'everyone who commits sin is a slave to sin' (John 8:34); but 'if the Son sets you free, you will be free indeed' (John 8:36).

The reason for redemption—God's glory

But why does God intervene to save his people in this way? He is under no obligation to do so, and they are not in any position to require him to do so. In fact, he has already intimated the reasons to Moses before this, in Exodus 6:5–8:

Moreover, I have heard the groaning of the people of Israel whom the Egyptians hold as slaves, and I have remembered my covenant. Say therefore to the people of Israel, 'I am the LORD, and I will bring you out from under the burdens of the Egyptians, and I will deliver you from slavery to them, and I will redeem you with an outstretched arm and with great acts of judgement. I will take you to be my people, and I will be your God, and you shall know that I am the LORD your God, who has brought you out from under the burdens of the Egyptians. I will bring you into the land that I swore to give to Abraham, to Isaac and to Jacob. I will give it to you for a possession. I am the LORD.'

In this passage God identifies at least four reasons for redeeming his people:

First, *He does it for his own glory.* 'Say to the people of Israel, "I am the LORD".' Ultimately, that is the reason why he is going to act. He will send plagues on the land as a precursor to bringing his people out so that 'the Egyptians will know that I am the LORD' (Exodus 7:5). He reiterates that purpose at Exodus 10:2 ('that you may tell in the hearing of your son and of your grandson how I have dealt harshly with the Egyptians and what signs I have done among them, *that you may know that I am the LORD*'). And it is explicit in Exodus 12:12: 'I will pass through the land of Egypt that night and I will strike all the firstborn in the land of Egypt, both man and beast; and on all the gods of Egypt I will execute judgements. *I am the LORD.*'

So, the might and glory and supremacy of the God of Israel are to be pitted against the impotence and indignity and transience of the gods of Egypt. For at last, this is not a battle between Pharaoh and Moses, between the Israelites and the Egyptians; it is a battle between gods, between the supreme God of Heaven and the pretended gods of earth. It is a spiritual issue, and spiritual truths are to be vindicated in it; God will have the glory as he redeems his people.

In a similar way, Paul presses home to the Ephesians that this is precisely the nature of their salvation: 'In love he predestined us for adoption as sons through Jesus Christ, according to the purpose of his will, *to the praise of his glorious grace,* with which he has blessed us in the Beloved. In him we have redemption through his blood …' (Ephesians 1:5–7). Just as the purpose of creation was to display his glory, so the purpose of redemption is to display his glory. The Puritan Thomas Brooks says that 'the work of creation is in many ways admirable, yet not to be compared with the work of redemption, wherein the power, wisdom, justice, mercy and other divine attributes of God do much more shine forth'.[1] Redemption displays God's glory in a way that not even creation does.

Second, God does it *because of his mercy*. He heard the groaning of his people, and pitied them. He redeemed them not because of their numerical strength or importance, or anything else that was true of them; he did it simply because of his great love. God's sovereign mercy is the spring from which his saving activity rises. Later on, God will declare to Moses: 'I will be gracious to whom I will be gracious, and will show mercy on whom I will show mercy' (Exodus 33:19; cf. Romans 9:15). And the mercy which saves is the mercy which will continue to be shown to Israel, so that Moses can sing 'You have led in your steadfast love [or mercy] the people whom you have redeemed' (Exodus 15:13).

It is a theme of which the New Testament never tires:

But God, being rich in mercy, because of the great love with which he loved us, even when we were dead in our trespasses, made us alive together with Christ—by grace you have been saved—and raised us up with him and seated us with him in the heavenly places in Christ Jesus (Ephesians 2:4–6).

Or, as James puts it so provocatively, 'mercy triumphs over judgement' (James 2:13).

Third, *God redeems his people in order to honour his covenant*.

God says to Moses, 'I heard the groaning of the people ... and I have remembered my covenant' (Exodus 6:5, see also 2:24). The theme of God's covenant runs throughout Scripture. The promises given to Abraham, Isaac and Jacob revealed God's commitment to his people in covenant. Like a marriage contract, a covenant binds two parties together, formalizing a relationship between them. God is the God of his people; Israel is a people for God. The covenant was articulated when man sinned (in Genesis 3:15), again after the flood (in Genesis 9:8–17), and again in God's call to Abraham:

I will make of you a great nation, and I will bless you and make your name great, so that you will be a blessing. I will bless those who bless you, and him who dishonours you I will curse, and in you all the families of the earth shall be blessed (Genesis 12:2–3).

Each successive, epoch-making revelation of the covenant promise built on previous revelation, expanded on it, and drove the purpose of God's salvation forward, until Christ, the mediator of the covenant of God's grace with sinners, appeared. Covenant language appears everywhere in the Bible; indeed, Paul tells us explicitly that the reason Jesus died was so that the blessing of Abraham would come on the whole world (see Galatians 3:14f).

So it is God's commitment to his covenant that drives forward the work of redemption. Previously revealed promises and earlier verbal commitments are invoked as the supreme reason why God's grace is extended to Israel in bondage. The concept of covenant is older than Moses and the giving of the law. As John Murray puts it, 'the deliverance of Israel from Egypt and the bringing of them into the land of promise is in fulfilment of the covenant promise to Abraham respecting the possession of the land of Canaan'.[2] These are not different dispensations, but different castings and administrations of the one covenant of grace, the revelation of which serves to unfold in a progressive manner the commitment of God to save sinners.

Finally, *God redeems his people in order to make them his own.* God says, 'I will take you out and you will be a people for me.' In other words, he redeems them because of his commitment to the covenant; they are redeemed in order to be committed to that same covenant. The result of the redemption is that they are no longer their own: they must serve God. That is the exchange: the yoke of Egypt for the yoke of God. But, as God incarnate puts it, 'his yoke is easy' (Matthew 11:30). True freedom is to be found in exchanging the service of Egypt for the service of God.

The means of redemption—substitution
So how are Israel redeemed out of Egypt?

God reveals his glory in a dramatic series of judgements on Egypt, culminating in death. The firstborn in Egypt's homes must die. But God's people can be redeemed by following God's plan. If they put a lamb to death, sprinkling its blood on their homes, that death will be accepted in substitution, and they will be free. But not any lamb would do.

First, the lamb had to be perfect: 'without blemish, a male a year old'

(Exodus.12:5). Nothing other than an unblemished, healthy lamb would make a fitting offering to a holy and righteous God. Malachi 1:8 is a rebuke to those who offer blemished animals to the Lord which they would not offer to anyone else.

Second, the lamb had to be their own. It was to be kept in their homes for four days. This gave an opportunity for everyone to prepare. No one need be caught off guard. Ample opportunity was given. The lamb was to share the home of those who would be saved under its blood.

Third, the lamb had to be killed. The curse which would fall on Egypt would either slay the firstborn or be realized in the death of the lamb. To spare the lamb was to slay themselves. It was not enough to have a lamb— there had to be death, symbolized by bloodshed, and the sprinkling of the blood symbolized the transmuting of the punishment away from the people to the substitute.

In all of this, the sacrificial, substitutionary death of Christ was foreshadowed. As the prophet said, he was taken like a lamb for slaughter (Isaiah 53:7); as John tells us, the Lamb on Mount Zion is the one whose death has atoned for God's people (John 1:36; Revelation 7:14; 14:1; 22:3). But perhaps Peter encapsulates the thought best when he says that *'you were ransomed … with the precious blood of Christ, like that of a lamb without blemish or spot'* (1 Peter 1:19). Jesus is the sinless One, the only fitting offering on our behalf. He is the one made flesh, who dwelt among us. And he is the one who was slain. No other ground of our release from sin's captivity is possible. We cannot liberate ourselves. We remain slaves unless we trust absolutely in the death of the substitute for us.

The purpose of redemption—service

Why did God redeem his people? What object does he have in view? The answer to this is supplied in the promise God made to Moses in Exodus 3:12: 'When you have brought the people out of Egypt, *you shall serve God on this mountain.*' It is emphasized again in the words Moses speaks to Pharaoh in Exodus 4:22–3: 'Thus says the LORD, Israel is my firstborn son, and I say to you, "Let my son go that he may serve me." If you refuse to let him go, behold, I will kill your firstborn son.' Again, just before the first plague, in which Egypt's rivers will be turned to blood, Moses is to repeat the charge to Pharaoh in this way: 'Let my people go, that they may serve me in the wilderness' (Exodus 7:16).

Israel, freed from slavery, is to serve God as God's son—and that is the whole purpose of redemption. With redemption comes release, and with freedom the opportunity to serve the Lord. The New Testament makes the same connections. Romans 6:22 says, 'But now that you have been set free from sin and have become slaves of God, the fruit you get leads to sanctification and its end, eternal life.' Similarly, Paul describes the conversion of the Thessalonians as a turning 'from idols to serve the living and true God' (1 Thessalonians 1:9). God creates a community of servants, who will yield everything to God here as their reasonable service (or 'spiritual worship'—Romans 12:1), and who will look forward to heaven, where it is said of the Lamb that 'his servants will worship him' (Revelation 22:3).

The consequences of redemption—salvation

So, finally, let's look at some of the consequences of redemption in the lives of God's people. There are five things that they had as a result of God bringing them out of Egypt.

LIBERTY

They were free at last! After four centuries of slavery, they finally knew what it was to be set free. It is interesting to note how God served to remind them of this when he gave them various laws regarding their own slaves. In Exodus 21:1–6, for example, they are to offer their slaves their freedom in the seventh year. Similarly, the fourth commandment has a particular clause respecting the condition of slaves; according to Deuteronomy 5:15, one of the reasons for the fourth commandment is:

You shall remember that you were a slave in the land of Egypt, and the LORD your God brought you out from there with a mighty hand and an outstretched arm. Therefore the LORD your God commanded you to keep the Sabbath day.

So the Sabbath is a sign of liberty, a sign that God remembers the slaves and acts in the interests of the slaves. He offers freedom and life.

OBEDIENCE

Second, the Israelites had a new motive for obeying God. The ten commandments are prefaced by the words 'I am the LORD your God, who brought you out of the land of Egypt, out of the house of slavery' (Deuteronomy 5:6). Their freedom is not a freedom *from* obedience but *to* obedience. As the redeemed people of God, they worship God by delighting to do his will. They receive his law as the book of his covenant with them, and they pledge obedience (Exodus 24:7). He has fulfilled his role as the covenant Lord; they now fulfil theirs as the covenant servants.

WORSHIP

Third, the redeemed people worship. One of the first projects is the construction of the tabernacle, which occupies most of the last fourteen chapters of Exodus. They will sacrifice and offer to the Lord, singing his praise and honouring his name because they are his redeemed people. So the psalmist says:

Oh give thanks to the LORD, for he is good,
for his steadfast love endures forever!
Let the redeemed of the LORD say so,
whom he has redeemed from trouble
and gathered in from the lands,
from the east and from the west,
from the north and from the south (Psalm 107:1–3).

Why do sinners worship God? Why should those whose natural inclination is to self-will and self-interest praise the name of Jacob's God? It is because they have been redeemed. He did it. He created within them a desire for himself. A genuine, worshipping community is proof of the glorious grace of God.

GUIDANCE

Fourth, as the redeemed people of God they had a new guidance in their lives. That is very clear at the end of Exodus, which speaks of the glory of the Lord filling the tabernacle in a cloud and leading Israel onwards

(Exodus 40:34–38). Having redeemed his people, God pledged to guide them. Their lives now had purpose and direction. God never let them go, and never left them to themselves. This formed part of Moses' song of thanksgiving following the crossing of the Red Sea: 'You have led in your steadfast love the people whom you have redeemed; you have guided them by your strength to your holy abode' (Exodus 15:13). That is why Isaiah can confidently say to the people of God: 'the LORD will guide you continually' (Isaiah 58:11).

HOPE

Finally, having been released from Egypt, they are a hope-filled people. Bondage is behind them, better is before them. They are to follow on until God will fulfil promises covenanted to the patriarchs. Redemption is definitive and climactic; but it is only the beginning of pilgrimage.

Notes

1 **Thomas Brooks,** *Works,* V (1861–1867; reprinted Edinburgh: The Banner of Truth Trust, 1980) p. 353.
2 **John Murray,** *The Covenant of Grace* (London: The Tyndale Press, 1954), p. 20.

The wonder of inheritance

… the land that you are going over to possess is a land of hills and valleys, which drinks water by the rain from heaven, a land that the LORD your God cares for. The eyes of the LORD your God are always upon it, from the beginning of the year to the end of the year (Deuteronomy 11:11–12).

Reading through the Bible shows us the importance of the theme of the land. In the Old Testament, it is very significant. Even from the point of vocabulary, the theme is very prominent. One Old Testament scholar says that '"land" is the fourth most frequent noun or substantive in the Old Testament: it occurs 2,504 times. Statistically land is a more dominant theme than covenant.'[1]

After the exodus, the most defining moment in Israel's experience was her taking possession of the land of Canaan. We cannot do justice to the Bible's story without referring to this theme.

When God took his people out of Egypt, it was with one clear, long-term aim in view: to fulfil the promise made to Abraham that he would give a land to his people. That promise was clearly articulated in the covenant with Abraham: 'Go from your country and your kindred and your father's house *to the land that I will show you*' (Genesis 12:1). God's action in redeeming his people was to be remembered by them once they settled in another land: 'You shall observe this rite as a statute for you and for your sons for ever. And *when you come to the land that the LORD will give you*, as he has promised, you shall keep this service' (Exodus 12:24–25).

But forty years were to elapse before that promise was realized. During that time, under the leadership of Moses, God took his people through the wilderness. He gave them laws at Sinai, including instructions for the setting up of the tabernacle as a temporary place of worship, where he dwelt among his people. He also fed them with manna, a white, bread-like substance which covered the ground each day of the week but one, but which provided sufficient sustenance for their daily journey. In this way, God met all the needs of his people, physical and spiritual.

Moses, who had led God's people out of Egypt, would not, however, lead them into the land of promise. That honour was to belong to Joshua, one of only two people who would both leave Egypt and enter the land of Canaan. It was a new generation, under a new leadership, that would experience the fulfilment of the promise God had made to Abraham. The Book of Deuteronomy is a kind of farewell discourse by Moses, as he prepares the people for their entrance into the land of which he will catch a glimpse before his death (Deuteronomy 32:48–52). So, from the top of Mount Pisgah, where Moses would die and be buried, we are told that:

The LORD showed him all the land, Gilead as far as Dan, all Naphtali, the land of Ephraim and Manasseh, all the land of Judah as far as the western sea, the Negeb and the Plain, that is, the Valley of Jericho the city of palm trees, as far as Zoar. And the LORD said to him, 'This is the land of which I swore to Abraham, to Isaac and to Jacob, "I will give it to your offspring." I have let you see it with your eyes, but you shall not go over there' (Deuteronomy 34:1–4).

The story of Moses' successor is told in the Book of Joshua, which opens with a reaffirmation of this theme of the land. These are God's words to Joshua:

Moses my servant is dead. Now therefore, arise, go over this Jordan, you and all this people, *into the land* that I am giving to them, to the people of Israel. Every place that the sole of your foot will tread upon I have given to you, just as I promised to Moses (Joshua 1:2–3).

And so we come to one of the great defining, pivotal moments of the Bible story: the crossing of the River Jordan and the first days in the land of Canaan (Joshua 3–5). The details are awesome and staggering. The River Jordan marks the boundary of the land, and it is at a high-mark when the Israelites come to it (Joshua 3:15). The moment is holy; the people need to be consecrated for the occasion (Joshua 3:5). The first ones to cross the Jordan are the priests, carrying the Ark of the Covenant. As soon as their feet touch the waters of Jordan, the waters recede, allowing safe passage across the river:

Now the priests bearing the ark of the covenant of the LORD stood firmly on dry ground in the midst of the Jordan, and all Israel was passing over on dry ground until all the nation finished passing over the Jordan (Joshua 3:17).

Then, in one of the significant story-telling motifs of the book of Joshua, a cairn of stones taken from the bed of the river is set up as a memorial (Joshua 4:8–9; cf. further memorial cairns at 7:25–26 and 10:27). The action is complete. Israel has crossed the river. They are now in the land. And one of the consequences is this:

On that day the LORD exalted Joshua in the sight of all Israel, and they stood in awe of him just as they had stood in awe of Moses, all the days of his life (Joshua 4:14).

The land into which they have entered will become the theatre of God's redeeming activity. His saving work in both Old and the New Testament will focus to a large extent on the land of Israel. In a very real sense, therefore, the theme of the land becomes the background for subsequent Old Testament history and theology. It is important, therefore, as we try to bring the strands together—particularly of Old Testament history—together, to look, firstly, at the people's experience of living in the land of Canaan; secondly, at what their experience of the land symbolized for them; and finally at what the land represented as part of God's ongoing and unfolding covenant revelation.

The experience of the land

There are four distinct elements to the experience of Israel in the land of Canaan.

First, there is *their possession of the land*. The realization of the dream had taken place when the tribes of Israel followed the priests across the river. Egypt was gone. The wilderness was behind them. The people of God were finally settled in a place which was theirs.

And, constantly, the refrain throughout the Old Testament is that this is a grace-gift on the part of God to his people. It is the land God has given them (Genesis 12:7; Leviticus 14:34; Numbers 11:12; Deuteronomy 1:8). It is the land which God will secure for them, by driving out the inhabitants. The Ark of the Covenant, causing the waters to recede and allow a safe passage over Jordan, was to be a sign 'that the living God is among you and that he will without fail drive out from before you the Canaanites, the Hittites, the Hivites, the Perizzites, the Girgashites, the Amorites and the Jebusites' (Joshua 3:10). And it is the land whose bounty is secured by God for his people, so that in it they will eat 'the fruit of vineyards and olive orchards that you did not plant' (Joshua 24:13).

Some people raise a question of morality over this: how could God send his people into Canaan to dispossess those who dwelt there and occupy it themselves? Part of the answer to that question lies in the wickedness of the Canaanites themselves. The covenant with Abraham included these promises:

Know for certain that your offspring will be sojourners in a land that is not theirs and will be servants there, and they will be afflicted for four hundred years. But I will bring judgement on the nation that they serve, and afterward they shall come out with great possessions. As for yourself, you shall go to your fathers in peace; you shall be buried in a good old age. And they shall come back here in the fourth generation, for the iniquity of the Amorites is not yet complete (Genesis 15:13–16).

The wickedness of the inhabitants of the land has now reached its height; God will dispossess them of their paradise, just as he dispossessed Adam of paradise at the beginning. As God's people possess the land, they experience the grace that saves, that chooses an inheritance for them, that allots their portion, that provides their needs, that speaks of God's unmerited favour and undeserved love. Of all the peoples of the world, he shows favour to none as he shows favour to Israel (Psalm 147:20). The reason why he does it is known only to him:

You are a people holy to the LORD your God. The LORD your God has chosen you to be a people for his treasured possession, out of all the peoples who are on the face of the earth. It was not because you were more in number than any other people that the

LORD set his love on you and chose you, for you were the fewest of all peoples, but it is because the LORD loves you and is keeping the oath that he swore to your fathers ... (Deuteronomy 7:6–8).

God's people rejoice in his grace, which works wonders for them, securing for them their inheritance and settling them in their land. It is the same grace that works still in the experience of his people. God still does wonderful things for them in Christ, all because of the sovereign glory of his undeserved love and favour and grace.

Second, there is *their occupation of the land*. The crossing of the Jordan is only the beginning. The Old Testament follows the history of God's people during the period of the judges, when the land is occupied by Israel as a confederation of tribes under the leadership of judges whom God raises up at various points to deliver his people out of trouble. Then there comes the period of the monarchy, when the land is governed by King Saul, King David and King Solomon before being divided into two kingdoms—Israel in the north and Judah in the south. The Bible history follows the story of these kings and dynasties to the fall of Jerusalem in 587BC.

Interwoven with these events are the ministries of the prophets in Israel and Judah. The prophets bring God's word to the people, reminding them of the fact that God has given them possession of the land:

It was I who brought you up out of the land of Egypt and led you forty years in the wilderness, to possess the land of the Amorite (Amos 2:10).

To sin against God in the land was to despise God's grace and to reject God's mercy and love:

In this also your fathers blasphemed me, by dealing treacherously with me. For when I had brought them into the land that I swore to give them, then wherever they saw any high hill or any leafy tree, there they offered their sacrifices and there they presented the provocation of their offering ... (Ezekiel 20:27–8).

And to a wayward people, God continued to bring words of hope, grace, mercy and forgiveness:

The LORD became jealous for his land and had pity on his people. The LORD answered and said to his people, 'Behold, I am sending to you grain, wine and oil, and you will be satisfied; and I will no more make you a reproach among the nations ... Fear not, O land; be glad and rejoice, for the LORD has done great things!' (Joel 2:18–19, 21).

The land, therefore, became the place where God ruled over his people, and where God spoke to his people. He governed them and he gave them his word. He was over them as their sovereign, and spoke to them as their Saviour.

It is still the experience of God's people that they experience and know their God as one who both governs and guides, rules and speaks. To be a follower of the Saviour is to belong to his covenant community, which acknowledges no king but Jesus, and no authority but his word.

Third, there is *their experience of the loss of the land*. Nebuchadnezzar of Babylon invades the holy land and destroys Jerusalem. Many of the inhabitants of Israel and Judah are deported to Babylon, and remain captive there for the best part of two generations. Jeremiah delivers God's word of judgement:

Because you have not obeyed my words, behold, I will send for all the tribes of the north, declares the LORD, and for Nebuchadnezzar the king of Babylon, my servant, and I will bring them against this land and its inhabitants, and against all these surrounding nations. I will devote them to destruction, and make them a horror, a hissing and an everlasting desolation. Moreover, I will banish from them the voice of mirth and the voice of gladness, the voice of the bridegroom and the voice of the bride, the grinding of the millstones and the light of the lamp. This whole land shall become a ruin and a waste, and these nations shall serve the king of Babylon seventy years (Jeremiah 25:8–11).

It was not a message without hope; Jeremiah would go on to say that after seventy years God would punish Babylon; but in the interim Babylon would be the rod of his chastisement, the means by which he would deal with the treachery of his people.

The experience of this loss is registered in passages such as Psalm 137, where, weeping by Babylon's rivers, the captives remember Zion, and in Daniel 6:10, where Daniel, one of the captives, makes it his daily routine to pray to God, facing Jerusalem. Interestingly, as Daniel analyses the seventy-year prophecy of Jeremiah (see Daniel 9:2), God reveals to him that even the captivity has its purpose in God's plan of salvation. Yet the experience is still devastating. What must have gone through Amos's heart as God commissioned him to bring the following message to his people?

Your wife shall be a prostitute in the city, and your sons and your daughters shall fall by the sword, and your land shall be divided up with a measuring line; you yourself shall die in an unclean land, and Israel shall surely go into exile away from its land (Amos 7:17).

The blessing which Israel was to experience in the land was conditional upon the obedience of the people to their God and to his word. The gift of the land was entirely unconditional—it was a gift of grace. Yet no one could assume that God would ignore the rebellious disobedience of his people. Indeed, it was in grace that, time and again, God sent his word and his call to his people; but they refused to hear and to obey. Of the northern kingdom, 2 Kings 18:11–12 tells us that

The king of Assyria carried the Israelites away to Assyria and put them in Halah and on the Habor the river of Gozan and in the cities of the Medes because they did not obey the voice of the LORD their God but transgressed his covenant, even all that Moses the servant of the LORD commanded. They neither listened nor obeyed.

And of the southern kingdom of Judah, 2 Chronicles 36:14–16 summarizes:

All the officers of the priests and the people likewise were exceedingly unfaithful, following all the abominations of the nations. And they polluted the house of the LORD that he had made holy in Jerusalem. The LORD, the God of their fathers, sent persistently to them by his messengers, because he had compassion on his people and on his dwelling place. But they kept mocking the messengers of God, despising his words and scoffing at his prophets, until the wrath of the LORD rose against his people, until there was no remedy.

It is a hard lesson to learn, but the experience of the people in the land teaches it so clearly: sin brings loss, and forfeits our right to any blessing. God warned; but they did not listen. Their past did not save them when they sinned in the present. The land they had been given was taken from them. God is not mocked: not then, not now.

But, finally, God's people experienced *the restoration of the land*. It was given back to them. Cyrus, the king of Persia, overthrew Babylon and granted the Jewish people the opportunity to return. The books of Ezra and Nehemiah tell of the return to the land, the rebuilding of the city and the temple, and the restoration of God's people in their own place. It was a marvellous, unique event. Psalm 126 declared that 'when the LORD restored the fortunes of Zion, we were like those who dream ... The LORD has done great things for us; we are glad'. And Jeremiah, who prophesied so clearly and solemnly about the captivity, also declared that the glory of the restoration would eclipse even the glory of the redemption:

Therefore, behold, the days are coming, declares the LORD, when they shall no longer say, 'As the LORD lives who brought up the people of Israel out of the land of Egypt', but 'As the LORD lives who brought up and led the offspring of the house of Israel out of the north country and out of all the countries where he had driven them.' Then they shall dwell in their own land (Jeremiah 23:7).

Zechariah portrays God as rousing his people, calling them to leave Babylon and return home:

Up! Up! Flee from the land of the north, declares the LORD. For I have spread you abroad as the four winds of the heavens, declares the LORD. Up! Escape to Zion, you who dwell with the daughter of Babylon. For thus said the LORD of hosts, after his glory sent me to the nations who plundered you, for he who touches you touches the apple of his eye: 'Behold, I will shake my hand over them, and they shall become plunder for those who served them. Then you will know that the LORD of hosts has sent me. Sing and rejoice. O daughter of Zion, for behold, I come and I will dwell in your midst, declares the LORD. And many nations shall join themselves to the LORD in that day, and shall be my people. And I will dwell in your midst, and you shall know that the LORD of hosts has sent me to you. And the LORD will inherit Judah as his portion in the holy land, and will again choose Jerusalem' (Zechariah 2:6–12).

Thus it is evident that God's covenant commitment extends to his jealousy for the land, as the theatre of his saving acts. In possession, occupation, loss and restoration, the people of God are the objects of God's saving and loving grace. He is moulding them, shaping them, revealing himself to them. Above all, he is showing himself faithful to the covenant undertaking which Moses had to declare to God's people in bondage:

I am the LORD, and I will bring you out from under the burdens of the Egyptians, and I will deliver you from slavery to them, and I will redeem you with an outstretched arm and with great acts of judgement. I will take you to be my people, and I will be your God, and you shall know that I am the LORD your God, who has brought you out from under the burdens of the Egyptians. I will bring you into the land that I swore to give to Abraham, to Isaac, and to Jacob. I will give it to you for a possession. I am the LORD (Exodus 6:6–8).

The symbolism of the land

But what did this experience of the land mean to God's people? What did it symbolize to Israel in the Old Testament?

First, *it spoke of God's promise, and his faithfulness to his covenant commitment*. The whole tenor of the opening books of the Bible is of God's fulfilling his promise. To use Martens' phraseology, 'the schema or plot of the literature from Genesis to Joshua is a promise-fulfilment schema'.[2] Land was lost with the exclusion of man from Eden; land was promised with the call of Abraham to leave Ur; the promise was re-issued on the eve of exodus from Egypt and throughout the ministry of Moses; the promise was fulfilled and verified with the experience of possession and occupation of the land. Everything about the land spoke of promise.

The corollary of this, of course, is that God's people were called to have faith in his promise. Hence the writer to the Hebrews can say that

By faith Abraham obeyed when he was called to go out to a place that he was to receive as an inheritance. And he went out, not knowing where he was going … for he was looking forward to the city that has foundations, whose designer and builder is God (Hebrews 11:8, 10).

The people of God were to be a people of faith. All that God gave them in the land showed that his promise was true, his word dependable, and their God faithful.

Second, *the land spoke of God's provision*. It was to be a land of plenty: To use the oft-repeated phrase of the Old Testament, it was to be a land 'flowing with milk and honey' (Exodus 3:8, 17; 13:5; 33:3; Leviticus 20:24; Deuteronomy 6:3; 11:9). Or, in other words:

The LORD your God is bringing you into a good land, a land of brooks of water, of fountains and springs, flowing out in the valleys and hills, a land of wheat and barley, of vines and fig trees and pomegranates, a land of olive trees and honey, a land in which you will eat bread without scarcity, in which you will lack nothing; a land whose stones are iron, and out of whose hills you can dig copper. And you shall eat and be full, and you shall bless the LORD your God for the good land he has given you (Deuteronomy 8:7–10).

In the words of one commentator, this passage contains the most vivid portrayal of the land, 'picturing its natural richness with an accumulation of its features. All is in contrast with the desert. In place of the hand-to-mouth sustenance provided by the manna, the means of livelihood will be present regularly and in abundance … the theme of land becomes here an ideal, or dream, of plenty'.3

The failure to trust in God's provision becomes an occasion of God's anger burning against Israel, as recorded in Numbers 14. Preferring to listen to the ten spies who had spied out the land and emphasized only the difficulties, the people are accused of despising God. As a result, they will perish in the wilderness, apart from Joshua and Caleb, who brought a good report back (Numbers 14:38). Eventually, when Joshua did lead the people into Canaan, the manna of the desert stopped, and 'they ate of the fruit of the land of Canaan that year' (Joshua 5:12).

There is an interesting link here with the Garden of Eden, where all the fruit except that of one tree was given to Adam and Eve for food. The eating of the forbidden fruit led to expulsion from the garden and the loss of the permitted fruit. Now, grace has acted to restore what sin took away; once again, there will be fruit. Now, it will be the fruit of Canaan. God supplies all the needs of his people. No one perishes who trusts in him.

Third, *the land symbolized God's protection of his people.* He had always promised to be with them. But now he is taking them to a land where his care for them will be evident. His eyes are on the land from year's beginning to year's end (Deuteronomy 11:12), and, conditional on their obedience, God promises protection in the following ways:

No one shall be able to stand against you. The LORD your God will lay the fear of you and the dread of you on all the land that you shall tread (Deuteronomy 11:25).

The LORD will cause your enemies who rise against you to be defeated before you. They shall come out against you one way and flee before you seven ways (Deuteronomy 28:7).

The LORD your God will put all these curses on your foes and enemies who persecuted you … when you obey the voice of the LORD your God (Deuteronomy 30:7, 10).

God's faithfulness to his covenant threat is seen in the withdrawal of that protection when the land sins against him. Disobedience would result in loss: 'you shall be plucked off the land that you are entering to take possession of it' (Deuteronomy 28:63). The rebellion of the people led to God modifying his promise to drive out the nations by leaving some nations to afflict Israel longer in the land (Judges 2:20–22). And, ultimately, the sin of the people led to the loss of the land at the time of the exile.

But the land was peculiarly the land under God's care. It was his vineyard, which he looked after constantly so that no one would destroy it (Isaiah 27:2–3). It symbolized the fact that covenant love erected a wall of protection and of care around covenant people. In God there is protection and there is strength.

Fourth, *the experience of the land represented God's principle of obedience and faithfulness.* Throughout the Old Testament, there is a connection made between law and land, between possession of the promised inheritance and a lifestyle of obedience. Thus we have phrases such as 'These are the statutes and rules that you shall be careful to do in the land that the LORD, the God of your fathers, has given you to possess, all the days that you live on the earth' (Deuteronomy 12:1). As Martens puts it, 'human conduct and behaviour are understood to have a bearing on land, and conversely land occupancy demands a particular quality of lifestyle'.4 There were laws to keep, associated with religious festivals and worship, moral behaviour and obedience, and care and protection of their environment. The people of God were in no doubt that their enjoyment of the blessings associated with the land was an unconditional gift, with conditional aspects to it.

The same is true of us today. What does it mean to be a Christian? It means to have experienced the grace of God, unmerited, unearned, free; yet demanding of us that we listen to the voice of God in order to enjoy the fruit of the land. Or, as Moses puts it:

And when the LORD your God brings you into the land that he swore to your fathers, to Abraham, to Isaac, and to Jacob, to give you—with great and good cities that you did not build, and houses full of all good things that you did not fill, and cisterns that you did not dig, and vineyards and olive trees that you did not plant—and when you eat and are full, then take care lest you forget the LORD, who brought you out of the land of Egypt, out of the house of slavery. It is the LORD your God you shall fear. Him you shall serve and by his name you shall swear. You shall not go after other gods, the gods of the peoples who are around you—for the LORD your God in your midst is a jealous God— lest the anger of the LORD your God be kindled against you, and he destroy you from off the face of the earth (Deuteronomy 6:10–15).

The typology of the land

But what does this mean for us now that Christ has come, and now that we can enjoy the blessings of the new covenant? In what sense are we inheritors of the land? The promise to Abraham was that the possession of the land would belong to his offspring for ever (Genesis 13:15). If we are the children of Abraham, and heirs of the promise (Galatians 3:29), what does the land of Canaan mean for us?

One thing is fundamentally important, and has important consequences for our understanding of much in the Old Testament. It is the fact that although the promises were fulfilled literally to Israel, they had an ultimate, spiritual aspect to them. So, for example, when God promised to be present with his people in the Old Testament tabernacle, that promise was literally fulfilled. Moses built the tabernacle and God was with his people. But the promise awaited its ultimate, spiritual fulfilment, first with the coming of Christ, 'God with us' (Matthew 1:23), who 'tabernacled' among us (John 1:14); and it also awaits its final, eternal fulfilment in the coming of the day when the tabernacle of God will be with his people in heaven and he will dwell with them (Revelation 21:3). Because of that immediate/ultimate and literal/final fulfilment, we can say that the tabernacle functions in Scripture as a type both of Christ and of heaven.

The Old Testament experience of the land is the same. Literally, God's people experienced the promise. Yet, as Palmer Robertson reminds us, 'Throughout its history, Israel's experience with the land had the effect of placing the promise of it in the category of an old covenant shadow that would have to wait for the arrival of new covenant realities for its fulfilment'.5

So although Israel received the promise of the land, there is always the realization throughout the Word of God that it foreshadowed and represented something greater, something enduring, something ultimate. What is that something? Of what was the promise and possession of the land a type and foreshadowing?

First, in general terms, we can say *that the land represented all that is ours in Jesus Christ.* We have already become possessors of the land because Christ is ours. The reasoning of the apostle Paul is that 'all things are yours ... and you are Christ's and Christ is God's' (1 Corinthians 3:21–23). Indeed, Paul reasons that this *is* our inheritance:

In [Christ] we have obtained an inheritance ... In him you also, when you heard the word of truth, the gospel of your salvation, and believed in him, were sealed with the promised Holy Spirit, who is the guarantee of our inheritance until we acquire possession of it, to the praise of his glory (Ephesians 1:11, 13–14).

In other words, we have both acquired a spiritually rich inheritance in Christ, and been given the Holy Spirit as the pledge that we will have full possession of it one day.

But I think we can be more specific. In particular, the prophet Ezekiel ties the idea of the land to various themes that find their full expression in the gospel.

Second, the land *typified the new work that God would do in Christ*. In Ezekiel 33:28–29 the threat against the land is reiterated: the land will be desolate because of its sins. But in chapter 34, God promises restoration, and he does so under the imagery of the shepherd. This is his particular undertaking:

Behold I, I myself will search for my sheep and will seek them out. As a shepherd seeks out his flock when he is among his sheep that have been scattered, so will I seek out my sheep, and I will rescue them from all places where they have been scattered on a day of clouds and thick darkness … I will feed them with good pasture, and on the mountain heights of Israel shall be their grazing land. There they shall lie down in good grazing land, and on rich pasture they shall feed on the mountains of Israel (Ezekiel 34:11–12, 14).

This might simply be a poetic description of the restoration following the captivity, except that God promises to set one shepherd over his people in the land, 'my servant David, and he shall feed them … And I, the LORD, will be their God, and my servant David shall be prince among them' (Ezekiel 34:23–24). Yet David has been dead many years! He came, yet he is still to come. Just as David had governed God's people in the land of promise, so Jesus Christ would appear as the great prince, king and shepherd of his people. What God did for his people in the land of covenant blessing anticipated what he was to do in Christ.

Or, to put it otherwise, those who are in Christ's kingdom have entered the promised land. To the subjects of his kingdom he promises the possession of the whole earth as an inheritance (Matthew 5:5). Christ is our David. He is our Shepherd. He is our King. Spiritually, our possession of the covenant inheritance is ours because Christ is ours and we are in him.

Third, *the land typified the new birth*. Consider how Ezekiel runs these themes together in a prophecy concerning the restoration of God's people to Canaan:

> I will take you from the nations and gather you from all the countries and bring you into your own land. I will sprinkle clean water on you, and you shall be clean from all your uncleannesses, and from all your idols I will cleanse you. And I will give you a new heart, and a new spirit I will put within you. And I will remove the heart of stone from your flesh and give you a heart of flesh. And I will put my Spirit within you, and cause you to walk in my statutes and be careful to obey my rules. You shall dwell in the land that I gave to your fathers, and you shall be my people, and I will be your God (Ezekiel 36:24–28: cf. 11:14–21).

In this passage, the prophet is running together themes regarding the restoration to the land and the spiritual relationship of God to his people. He is not teaching that everyone who returns from Babylon to Canaan is in a right relationship with God, nor is he teaching that to be in a right relationship means literal occupation of the land. But he is defining the idea of land possession in terms of regeneration. So although the prophecy functions at one level literally—God was going to turn desolate Canaan into a new Eden (Ezekiel 36:35)—at another level he is speaking about the ultimate realities of his work of grace in the lives of his people. We 'possess the land' when we receive a new heart, are made new people, are born again.

Finally, the *experience of the land foreshadows the reality of resurrection*. Ezekiel 37 speaks about dry bones in the valley coming to life. The condition of the bones in the valley is like that of Israel in exile, saying 'our bones are dried up and our hope is lost' (Ezekiel 37:11). But God's response is:

> I will open your graves and raise you from your graves, O my people. And I will bring you into the land of Israel. And you shall know that I am the LORD when I open your graves and raise you from your graves, O my people. And I will put my Spirit within you, and you shall live, and I will place you in your own land. Then you shall know that I am the LORD (Ezekiel 37:12–14).

Just as the restoration to the land would be like a resurrection from the dead, so the resurrection of the dead will be for us as a restoration of the land. Here we are not so much in the wilderness as in exile; not journeying towards the promised land so much as removed from it. But one day graves will open, we will return to our Eden, and experience the blessing of resurrection.

However, in all of this, let's remind ourselves of the one crucial difference between Israel's literal possession of the land inheritance and our spiritual possession of the blessings of the gospel. In Christ we are safe. Nothing he gives us can be taken from us, and we cannot be lost either. Here is what the apostle Peter wrote:

Blessed be the God and Father of our Lord Jesus Christ! According to his great mercy, he has caused us to be born again to a living hope through the resurrection of Jesus Christ from the dead, *to an inheritance that is imperishable, undefiled, and unfading,* kept in heaven for you, who by God's power are being guarded through faith for a salvation ready to be revealed in the last time (1 Peter 1:3–5).

The fulfilment of the promise—Israel's occupation of Canaan and their experiences there as God's covenant people—opened the possibility of even greater fulfilment. Now, in Christ, Paradise has been regained. We possess the land. We have the inheritance. The first instalment has been given us by the Holy Spirit. But even greater blessing lies ahead. There is a new heaven and a new earth awaiting us. On that day, we will truly experience the blessing of the land that flows with milk and honey!

Notes

1   **Elmer A. Martens,** *God's Design* (Grand Rapids, MI: Baker, 1986) p. 103–104.

1   Ibid. p. 104.

2   **J.G. McConville,** *Deuteronomy* (Leicester: Apollos, 2002), p 170.

3   **Martens,** *God's Design,* p. 114.

4   **O.P. Robertson,** *The Israel of God* (Phillipsburg, NJ: Presbyterian and Reformed, 2000), p. 13.

The wonder of incarnation

Everything written about me in the Law of Moses and the Prophets and the Psalms must be fulfilled (Luke 24:44).

This is my Son, my Chosen One (Luke 9:35).

We come to the fourth of the 'wonders' of the Bible's world—the fourth pivotal point on which the Bible's storyline hangs. From another point of view, the fourth point out of seven is, of course, the central point, and this central point is taking us to the very heart of the Bible's story, and to the very heart of the gospel.

Or, to put it another way, we could ask: what is the Bible for? Why does it exist? What is the purpose of its literature, its histories, poems and epistles? What is the point which is served by this collection of ancient literature and wisdom? The answer is—JESUS CHRIST. The purpose of this collection of writings is to introduce us to the one in whom there is life. John makes this clear in his Gospel:

These are written so that you may believe that Jesus is the Christ, the Son of God, and that by believing you may have life in his name (John 20:31).

We could put the question differently and ask, 'What is the gospel about? What is at the heart of the good news of salvation? What is at the core of our theological position? What is the central aspect of all that has ever been written, in two thousand years of church reflection and thought? What is the message of salvation?' It is JESUS CHRIST. There was a man in the New Testament who asked what is arguably the most important question in the world: 'What must I do to be saved?' There is only one answer to this question: 'Believe in the Lord Jesus, and you will be saved, you and your household' (Acts 16:30–31). Or, as Peter puts it,

This Jesus is the stone that was rejected by you, the builders, which has become the cornerstone. And there is salvation in no one else, for there is no other name under heaven given among men by which we must be saved (Acts 4:11–12).

For the New Testament church. the central theme of the Bible is JESUS, and the core message of the gospel is JESUS. The wonder is that this unique person is found among men and that he has come to save.

Our knowledge about Jesus comes primarily from the Gospel records of the New Testament. These do not profess to be modern biographies, giving every detail of his development, maturity, life and work. On John's admission, for example, Jesus did many things which have not been recorded (John 20:30). But they do purport to be accurate; Luke tells us, in the preface to his Gospel, that 'it seemed good to me also, having followed all things closely for some time past, to write an orderly account for you, most excellent Theophilus, that you may have certainty concerning the things you have been taught' (Luke 1:3–4).

Some scholars have argued in the past that the Gospels were written by the early church to advance the message of the church; therefore, so the argument goes, we cannot rely on these writings for historical accuracy. But it is precisely because the writings were ideological—written to serve a particular purpose—that we can rely on the history. Craig Blomberg puts it like this: 'Some falsely assume that what is told for theological purposes is less likely to be historical than is a mere recitation of facts. Indeed, often the opposite is the case, as people passionately committed to a cause want the facts to be known.'[1]

The example Blomberg cites is the history of the Holocaust—Jewish historians had a very clear purpose in writing the events afterwards, not just to recite historical facts, but also to win sympathy and reach a determination not to repeat the history. In the same way, the writers of the Gospels had no wish to falsify the record in the interests of their message. The message and the method were intertwined and closely related.

So, when we look at the texts themselves, the authors and the dates of writing, the intentions of the authors, the literary types and the external evidence, we can say that there are good historical grounds to assert the trustworthiness of the Gospel records. They are our window into the facts concerning the life of Jesus Christ on earth.

But in order to understand that life and its purpose, we also need the New Testament letters. The evangelists—the Gospel writers—tell us the details of the life and death of Jesus, while the apostles—the letter writers—explain the meaning and significance of these events for us.

Some scholars have argued that Christianity in its present form owes its origin to Paul's religion, as if that religion had nothing to do with Jesus of Nazareth. Often the teachings of Jesus and those of Paul are set off against each other, as if they were two entirely different forms of faith and worship. Yet nothing could be further from the truth. This is the conclusion to which J. Gresham Machen came in his study of Paul's faith:

The religion of Paul was not founded upon a complex of ideas derived from Judaism or from paganism. It was founded upon the historical Jesus. But the historical Jesus upon whom it was founded was not the Jesus of modern reconstruction but the Jesus of the whole New Testament and of Christian faith; not a teacher who survived only in the memory of His disciples, but the Saviour who after His redeeming work was done still lived and could still be loved.[2]

In other words, what Paul and the other New Testament writers do is to cast light for us on why Jesus did what he did, so that in our differing contexts and times we too might be followers of Jesus Christ.

On one occasion, Jesus and three of his followers were on a mountain. His glory was displayed before them, so that his whole appearance seemed to change. We call this his 'transfiguration', a word that means that his external appearance was changed. We are going to use Luke's account of this event, in Luke chapter 9, as a window into our study of the great, central moment of salvation and redemption history that we call the incarnation, when Christ came to dwell on earth among men. The transfiguration was of crucial importance for the apostles. Peter, James and John were with Jesus when it occurred. Peter refers to the event in 2 Peter 1:16–18:

For we did not follow cleverly devised myths when we made known to you the power and coming of our Lord Jesus Christ, but we were eyewitnesses of his majesty. For when he received honour and glory from God the Father. and the voice was borne to him by the Majestic Glory, 'This is my beloved Son, with whom I am well pleased', we ourselves heard this very voice borne from heaven, for we were with him on the holy mountain.

It was the fact of his being an eyewitness that enabled Peter to draw the attention of his readers to the authority and inerrancy of his message. Peter's argument is: God bore witness to the glory of Christ, we were there when it happened, to hear it for ourselves, therefore you can trust what Jesus says.

Similarly, the apostle John was greatly influenced by the occasion. When John says 'We have seen his glory, glory as of the only Son from the Father' (John 1:14), he may well be referring to this point in his life. It is in his Gospel that John speaks of Jesus as the word who 'became flesh', which is the meaning of 'incarnation'. The opening words of John's first letter could apply well to the transfiguration experience:

That which was from the beginning, which we have heard, which we have seen with our eyes, which we have looked upon and have touched with our hands, concerning the word of life—the life was made manifest, and we have seen it, and testify to it and proclaim to you the eternal life, which was with the Father and was made manifest to us—that which we have seen and heard we proclaim also to you, so that you too may have fellowship with us; and indeed our fellowship is with the Father and with his Son Jesus Christ (1 John 1:1–3).

So here was an event of which these apostles were eyewitnesses in order that they might be able to convey to us the certainty of the things that they had seen and heard. Our need is to ask: What does this transfiguration event tell us about Jesus? In particular, what does it tell us about WHO Jesus is? What does it tell us about WHAT Jesus did? And what does it tell us about HOW we are to respond to the incarnate Saviour?

JESUS—Who is he?

There are two striking elements to the Person central to this scene and central to the gospel story. The first is that he is with other people on a mountain. He has taken three friends to the mountain top in order to pray. From that perspective, he is like them, as surely as he is with them. Yet while he is praying, his appearance changes and his whole being shines. He is therefore unlike his companions. It is a voice from heaven that opens up the mystery to us: God the Father says of Jesus, 'This is my Son, my Chosen One'.

So this is our starting-point: *this Jesus is the Son of God*. Just as the Father attested him to be such at his baptism (Matthew 3:13–17; John 1:32–34), so he attests him now to be his Son. The whole record of the Gospels has the end in view that we will acknowledge the eternal deity of the Lord Jesus, believing him to be the Son of God. It is not that the Father is choosing this ordinary human being and adopting him as his Son, in the way in which he adopts us into his family; it is that the One whom the Father appointed to be the Saviour of the world was and is none other than his only begotten Son (John 3:16). When the fullness of the time had come, 'God sent forth his Son' (Galatians 4:4).

This is the measure of the Father's love for us—the measure of the fact that 'God is for us': 'He who did not spare his own Son but gave him up for us all, how will he not also with him graciously give us all things?' (Romans 8:32). The New Testament declares that the Saviour was the pre-existent Christ, antedating his appearance in the world, older than Abraham, and pre-dating the creation itself. He is the one who was in the beginning and who made all things (John 1:1ff), the one who alone is worthy of the title 'the image of the invisible God, the firstborn of all creation' (Colossians 1: 15), who is himself God, 'the radiance of the glory of God and the exact imprint of his nature' (Hebrews 1:3).

The transfiguration captures this in its description of what the disciples saw. His appearance changed. Moses and Elijah, figures from the Old Testament, stood with them as if Jesus had been their contemporary, too. They appeared in his glory. A cloud overshadowed them all. The scenes are reminiscent of the glory-cloud of the Old Testament; perhaps the whole scene was designed to reflect the presence of God's glory on Mount Sinai. At any rate, all these phenomena combine to demonstrate that there is a man here who is more than a man: someone in the world who is older, greater and bigger than the world.

At this particular moment, something happens to the humanity of this Person which shows that he is more than humanity: his human frame struggles to contain the glory which is his by native right. This is no stage-managed performance, in which lights shine on the star from the outside; this is a glimpse of what lies within.

Christ is the legitimate object of our worship precisely because he is God. John tells us that as the Son of God he is full of grace and truth (John 1:14). There is no need he cannot supply; no situation with which he cannot deal. It is at his feet we must bow, as Thomas did, saying 'My Lord and my God!' (John 20:28).

Yet the transfiguration makes sense only because this one, who is the Son of God, has come to dwell with men on the earth. He takes his companions with him to the mountain where he engages in prayer. He knows the language of dependence and submission, because he has entered our world. This one, who is the Word, has become flesh (John 1:14).

Our catechisms and creed have defined this further in two ways. Jesus, the Son of God, became man by taking to himself a true body and a reasonable soul. His body was prepared for him by God (Hebrews 10:5), and was especially created by the power of the Holy Spirit overshadowing Mary (Matthew 1:18; Luke 1:30–33). Free from sin and corruption, his was a true manhood. It knew all the restraints and constraints of our manhood, from tiredness to hunger, and was susceptible to temptation, pain and death.

Christ was also like us in all the range of our human emotions. He experienced love, compassion, anger, joy and sorrow. His heart was truly kind. He exemplified a life full of the fruit of the Holy Spirit (Galatians 5:22–23). As the New Testament puts it, 'he had to be made like his brothers in every respect' (Hebrews 2:17).

So the one who stands before us in the Bible as central to God's plan of salvation and central to the whole unfolding revelation of the Scriptures is both God and man, the Mediator, who is able to save sinners.

JESUS—What did he do?

But there is a second question that requires answering. Why did Jesus become man? What was it that he came to do?

That question is answered in the transfiguration passage in terms of the subject of the conversation between Jesus and the two figures who appear beside him, Moses and Elijah. These were two highly significant Old Testament characters. They had many things in common. They both appeared at strategic points in Old Testament history. They both performed miracles. They were the only men in the Old Testament to speak to God on Mount Sinai. Also, the end of their lives was in marked contrast to that of others; Moses died on the top of Mount Pisgah, and was buried by God himself (Deuteronomy 34:5–6). Elijah did not die, but was taken to heaven in a whirlwind, accompanied by horses and chariots of fire (2 Kings 2:11). These facts about their lives make them interesting, to say the least.

But their significance is surely deeper. The reality is that both of them represent the whole sweep of Old Testament prophecy. Consider what God says about Moses:

And there has not arisen a prophet since in Israel like Moses, whom the LORD knew face to face, none like him for all the signs and the wonders that the LORD sent him to do in the land of Egypt, to Pharaoh and to all his servants and to all his land, … (Deuteronomy 34:10–11).

And it was this Moses who had declared to God's people:

The LORD your God will raise up for you a prophet like me from among you, from your brothers—it is to him you shall listen … (Deuteronomy 18:15).

In other words, God communicated with his people through Moses, and that is what made him a prophet. Part of what he prophesied was that God would raise up a specific prophet who would be like Moses. Yet the Old Testament declares that such a prophet never arose in Israel. The world was still waiting for a prophet like Moses to appear.

Elijah bursts in on the scene of Old Testament history in 1 Kings 17, after a long period of prophetic silence. God once again communicates his word with signs and wonders. As Elijah confronts the wicked dynasty of Omri, there is a clash in Israel between the word of the covenant God and the rebellion of covenant-breaking Israel. Elijah passes the prophetic mantle on to Elisha after his departure to heaven—but that is not the last we hear of him. Malachi, the last of the Old Testament prophets, suddenly declares:

I will send you Elijah the prophet before the great and awesome day of the LORD comes (Malachi 4:5).

Jesus himself sheds light for us on the meaning of this when he says:

Truly, I say to you, among those born of women there has arisen no one greater than John the Baptist ... For all the Prophets and the Law prophesied until John, and if you are willing to accept it, he is Elijah who is to come (Matthew 11:11, 13–14).

What is going on here? Remarkably, the appearance of Moses and Elijah represents the beginning and the end of Old Testament prophecy. All that the Old Testament had waited for and predicted concerning God's work of salvation in the world was about to be fulfilled in one climactic moment.

What was that moment? Into what was it that the Old Testament prophets—to use Peter's own language—'searched and enquired carefully' (1 Peter 1:10)? What was it that the Spirit of Christ in them was indicating (1 Peter 1:11)? What was the subject of the conversation that these representatives of Old Testament prophecy had with Jesus on the mount of transfiguration? Luke tells us that they 'appeared in glory and spoke of his departure which he was about to accomplish at Jerusalem' (Luke 9:31). While Matthew (17:3) and Mark (9:4) say simply that they were talking with Jesus, Luke tells us what they were talking about.

Interestingly, they were talking about things that were yet to take place. Specifically, they were talking about events that would take place in Jerusalem. And particularly, they were talking about the *departure* or *exodus* of Jesus. This recalls the work of Moses, who was not only a prophet, but also the one by whom God led his people out of Egypt. All the redemptive glory of that exodus moment was focused now on the exodus of Jesus out of Jerusalem as the great substitutionary lamb, the liberator and redeemer of his people.

The work of Jesus was the work of a Redeemer. As the Son of Man, he came to give his life as a ransom for many (Mark 10:45). He came to do the will of his Father (John 6:38), and for him that will meant going to the cross to die. He became man, not merely for the sake of becoming man, but in order to die, to shed his blood and to redeem us from the law's curse (Galatians 3:13). The culminating song of the ages will be the song of the redeemed:

To him who loves us and has freed us from our sins by his blood and made us a kingdom, priests to his God and Father, to him be glory and dominion for ever and ever (Revelation 1:5–6).

This is what is at the heart of the Bible's teaching and the Christian gospel: there is an old rugged cross on which Jesus died, to reconcile us to God. The cross of Christ dominates the Gospel records of Jesus' life. For thirty-three years he lived, yet the events of the cross overshadow everything, and the Gospel writers want us to focus on the cross with a detail that is missing elsewhere. The Old Testament anticipated the death of Christ for our sins; the Gospels narrate that death, and the New Testament books go on to explain it. That's why we need to make Paul's words central to our telling of the Bible's gospel story:

Now I would remind you, brothers, of the gospel ... that Christ died for our sins in accordance with the Scriptures, that he was buried, that he was raised on the third day in accordance with the Scriptures (1 Corinthians 15:1–4).

'Christ died for our sins'. With these words Paul brings us to the very core of the message of the Bible and of our salvation. That Jesus died is an incontrovertible and undeniable fact of history. That Jesus died for our sins also makes it a fact of theology.

But it is a fact of theology which is often debated. What does it mean that Jesus died for our sins? The old view was the view of *penal substitution*—which means that Jesus died in our place (it was substitution) and to bear the penalty of our sins (it was penal).

But recent evangelical literature has suggested that this is not a biblical idea, but one which owes more to nineteenth century Western views about law and punishment. It has also been suggested that there are many other images of the cross in the Bible, such as Jesus as the victorious warrior (Colossians 2:14) or Jesus as our example (1 Peter 2:21), and if we focus on just one image we do not do justice to the others. Indeed, some writers have suggested that we need to create our own images of 'atonement' (a word which has been used to describe the totality of Jesus' saving work) for the twenty-first century.

Yet we cannot escape the Bible's insistence that at the heart of the cross-work of Jesus is, in fact, the glorious truth of penal substitution. The Son of Man gave his life as a ransom for many (Mark 10:45), he was the good shepherd who gave his life for his sheep (John 10:11,15). When he cried out, 'My God, my God, why have you forsaken me?' (Matthew 27:46), it was not because he was being punished for any sins he committed himself, but precisely because he was carrying *our* sins in his body to the cross (1 Peter 2:24). Like the lamb killed at the Passover for the redemption of Israel, Jesus is the lamb of God who takes away the sin of the world (John 1:29).

This is what makes the story of Jesus so compelling, and such good news. When we were unable to save ourselves, Jesus went to the cross for us: 'while we were still weak, at the right time Christ died for the ungodly' (Romans 5:6). This is what the Bible is about. It is what the gospel is about. It is where the story of God's salvation brings us. Our sins were 'imputed' or reckoned to the Jesus who had committed no sin, so that his righteousness might be imputed to us (2 Corinthians 5:21). That is what makes the gospel such glorious news, and the cross of Jesus the only resting-place for sinners.

In his *Pilgrim's Progress*, an allegory about Christian experience, the Puritan John Bunyan has his character, Christian, come to the cross. He has been carrying a huge burden of sin on his back, and nothing has freed him of it. But when he arrives at the cross, the burden rolls away, and Christian sings:

What a place is this!
Must here be the beginning of my bliss?
Must here the burden fall from off my back?

Must here the strings which bound it to me crack?
Blest cross! Blest sepulchre! Blest rather be
The Man that there was put to shame for me![3]

JESUS—How ought we to respond?

The transfiguration scene makes it clear that there is a right way and a wrong way to respond to Jesus. Peter's response was the wrong one. 'Let us make three tents, one for you and one for Moses and one for Elijah' (Luke 9:33). Luke adds that Peter did not know what he was saying; but Mark supplies the detail that 'they were terrified' (Mark 9:6).

Why did Peter suggest making three tents? Perhaps because he felt that the scene was reminiscent of the glory appearance of Sinai, which led to Moses building a tabernacle where the all-consuming glory could dwell among the Israelites. Perhaps he was afraid that the glory would consume them, and that they required a tabernacle covering. Certainly it was wrong to suggest that Moses and Elijah ought to be placed on the same level as Jesus. Peter forgot the uniqueness of the one whose glory they had seen.

But maybe Peter's response was wrong for an even more basic reason. Perhaps the problem was not that he wanted to build tabernacles, but that he wanted to do something. The most natural feeling on our part is that we must do something. The response of so many to the Christ of the gospel is that there is something they must do, something they must build.

But the correct response is altogether different. What does God say? 'This is my Son, my Chosen One; listen to him!' (Luke 9:35). Here at last, was the prophet the Old Testament could not supply: the one like Moses, with whom God spoke face to face, and to whom men ought to listen. Here, at last, was the one whose Spirit was in Moses and Elijah as they ministered the Word of God in their own day, anticipating the greater and fuller revelation of Christ to come. Here, at last, was the one in whom and through whom God would speak the final word of salvation to a lost and needy world.

And God's call to us is to listen to him, and to put our trust in his words. That's what Peter himself did, when he said, 'Lord, to whom shall we go? You have the words of eternal life' (John 6:68). That's what Mary did when she sat at Jesus' feet 'and listened to his teaching' (Luke 10:39).

That's what all do who live by faith, for faith means trusting solely and trusting wholly the promises of God in Jesus Christ. There is eternal life there, as there is forgiveness, hope and pardon. No one perishes who trusts in him.

May the Christ who is central to the gospel and central to the Bible story be the centre of our lives also!

Notes

1 **C. Blomberg,** *Jesus and the Gospels: An Introduction and Survey* (Leicester: Apollos, 1997), p. 93.

2 **J. G. Machen,** *The Origin of Paul's Religion* (Grand Rapids, MI: Eerdmans, 1925), p. 317.

3 *The Works of John Bunyan,* vol. 3 (Grand Rapids, MI: Baker Book House, 1977), p. 103.

The wonder of resurrection

He is not here for he has risen, as he said (Matthew 28:6).

God raised him on the third day (Acts 10:40).

We come to the fifth of the 'wonders' of the Bible's world—the fifth point without which the Bible's story would crumble: the fact and the doctrine of the physical resurrection of Jesus from the dead.

In 2004, Europe celebrated the 60th anniversary of D-Day. On 6 June 1944, allied troops stormed the beaches of Normandy, in German-occupied France. Many fell in doing so, but those who succeeded in their operation secured the liberation of Europe. The result was freedom and emancipation.

But D-Day did not end the war. By every assessment, it was crucial for securing victory. Yet VE-Day (Victory in Europe Day) was not called until the following year, in 1945. D-Day was not VE-Day, but without D-Day, without the deliverance which the Normandy landings effected, VE-Day would never have come. It was D-Day that guaranteed the end of the war, and the victory of the allies.

There is a sense in which the resurrection of Jesus, as a pivotal point of history, and the climactic point of revelation, functions in that way. Without it, no victory can be hoped for or anticipated. The resurrection did not secure the ultimate victory, but apart from it, there can be no victory. There is a sense in which, even two thousand years after the event, the war is still going on; but it is the resurrection of Jesus which guarantees the ultimate triumph of grace over sin, of God over Satan, of light over darkness, and of life over death.

Paul makes it clear that, to him, belief in the resurrection is the core Christian doctrine:

If Christ has not been raised, then our preaching is in vain and your faith is in vain. We are even found to be misrepresenting God, because we testified about God that he raised Christ, whom he did not raise, if it is true that the dead are not raised. For if the dead are not raised, not even Christ has been raised. And if Christ has not been raised, your faith is futile and you are still in your sins (1 Corinthians 15:14–17).

For Paul, those who deny the idea of resurrection are thereby denying the idea of Christ's bodily resurrection. And without his resurrection, the heart is torn out of the Christian message. It is vital, therefore, to establish both that the physical resurrection of Christ is a historical fact, and, consequently, a Christian doctrine. The two things go together. B.B. Warfield puts it this way:

The doctrines of Christianity are doctrines only because they are facts; and the facts of Christianity become its indispensable doctrines ... The resurrection of Christ is a fact, an external occurrence within the cognizance of men to be established by their testimony. And yet, it is the cardinal doctrine of our system: on it all other doctrines hang.[1]

The resurrection, therefore, represents the greatest revelation of God's plan of salvation in history. And because it is a fact of history, we can accept it as a doctrine of our faith.

Yet one problem remains. No one actually saw the body of Jesus Christ coming to life in the silence of the tomb. The nineteenth-century American pastor T.V. Moore asked: 'Why did not Christ rise in the presence of a crowd?'[2] After all, Christ's death and ascension were public spectacles, at which many people were present to witness the events. Yet the moment of resurrection was essentially private and hidden. There was no public display of life entering into the dead body of Jesus. Why did he not rise in the presence of a crowd?

The answer Moore himself supplies is that the fact of a secret resurrection places us all on the same level. No one is put at any advantage. All must take this doctrine on the basis of faith. The women must trust the angels; the disciples must trust the women; we must trust the disciples. We operate every day with the principle that truth may be established without immediate observation. Criminals are justly punished although no one saw the crime being committed, precisely because the evidence gives away the truth of the matter.

We, too, are asked to believe in the resurrection of Jesus although no one saw it happening. Yet faith does not mean it did not actually and literally happen. Believing it does not mean that it is not a historical fact. In fact, we believe in the resurrection because of evidence of a threefold nature.

The evidence

The first strand of evidence is *the expectation of the Old Testament*. Old Testament prophecy expected a Messiah. God's anointed one was to come. The seed of the woman was to bruise the serpent's head. For Jesus the Christ, the Messiah, that meant suffering and death, humiliation and ignominy and a cross.

But the same prophetic strand of expectation also anticipated the resurrection. Psalm 16, for example, spoke of one who could say

My heart is glad and my whole being rejoices;
my flesh also dwells secure.
For you will not abandon my soul to Sheol,
or let your holy one see corruption.
You make known to me the path of life;
in your presence there is fullness of joy;
at your right hand are pleasures for evermore (Psalm 16:9–11).

In Acts 2:23–33, Peter argues that because the grave of David can be located, David could not have been speaking about himself when he penned these words in the psalm. The one to whom God would reveal life, and whom he would not leave in the grave, was someone other than the author of the words. Peter's explanation is simple:

Being therefore a prophet, and knowing that God had sworn with an oath to him that he would set one of his descendants on his throne, [David] foresaw and spoke about the resurrection of the Christ, that he was not abandoned to Hades, nor did his flesh see corruption. This Jesus God raised up, and of that we all are witnesses (Acts 2:30–32).

The resurrection of Jesus, Peter is saying, ought to be no surprise. It was a major element in Old Testament teaching. The great servant song of Isaiah

52:13–53:12 spoke of a suffering Saviour, but also anticipated one whom God would exalt, one who 'shall be high and lifted up' (Isaiah 52:13), and whom God would 'divide ... a portion with the many, and he shall divide the spoil with the strong' (Isaiah 53:12). The language is that of a triumphant warrior, exulting in victory, and dividing the spoils of war.

In other words, the believers of the Old Testament, looking forward to the coming of Christ, had faith in the resurrection victory of the coming Messiah. He would die, but death would not hold him: 'he will swallow up death for ever' (Isaiah 25:8).

The second strand of evidence is the *eyewitness testimony of those who report to us in the Gospels* what they saw. It remains true that none of them witnessed the moment in which the resurrection took place, but what they did see was equally convincing.

They saw, first, that the grave in which Jesus was laid was now empty. The angel says, 'He is not here ... Come, see the place where he lay' (Matthew 28:6). Pilate had expressly set a watch, a seal and a guard on the grave in order to prevent anyone stealing Jesus' body and breaking in to the grave from the outside (Matthew 27:64–66). So, whatever the explanation for the vacant tomb, it is not that the body was stolen away. In fact, the only explanation is the one Pilate did not allow for: that it was possible for the grave to be broken out of, when it was impossible for it to be broken into!

The Gospels record the bewilderment of those who came to the grave not expecting it to be empty. Did they come to the wrong grave? Not if it had been specially marked by the imperial seal. Did they imagine it all? Not if Pilate's failure to produce the body can be explained. They saw what they saw: the grave was now unoccupied.

But, more than that, they saw Jesus himself. Paul says:

He appeared to Cephas, then to the twelve. Then he appeared to more than five hundred brothers at one time, most of whom are still alive, though some have fallen asleep. Then he appeared to James, then to all the apostles. Last of all, as to one untimely born, he appeared also to me (1 Corinthians 15:5–8).

Indeed, when a new apostle was to be chosen in place of Judas it was a requirement that he be 'a witness to his resurrection' (Acts 1:22). So the post-resurrection appearances of Jesus, according to Peter, were 'not to all the people but to us who had been chosen by God as witnesses, who ate and drank with him after he rose from the dead' (Acts 10:42). God established his truth in the mouth of these witnesses. They met and saw the living Lord, and we accept their testimony.

Third, there is the evidence *of the subsequent history of the church*. Put it this way: what was it that had the power to transform these scattered, doubting disciples into men who were bold and zealous for the Lord? What was it that turned their mourning into dancing? What was it that transformed their behaviour? What emboldened them to worship on the first day of the week instead of the seventh? What enabled them to go to death and seal the message of the gospel with their blood?

Nothing less than, and nothing other than, the resurrection of Jesus from the dead. None of their subsequent actions could have been possible had their Lord and Master remained dead. But the fact that he did not was what energized them and enabled them to go out and turn the world upside down.

Who raised up Jesus?

So, in the absence of any physical eyewitness testimony to the actual event of the resurrection, can we say with any certainty what happened? We can certainly speak about the resurrection in the light of several Scriptures.

Let's look, first, at *Christ's own statements about his resurrection*. He says:

> ... the Father loves me, because I lay down my life that I may take it up again. No one takes it from me, but I lay it down of my own accord. I have authority to lay it down, and I have authority to take it up again. This charge I have received from my Father (John 10:17–18).

For Jesus, the resurrection represented a further step in his obedience to the will of his Father. Although it is correct to speak of Christ's resurrection as the first step of his exaltation, it must be remembered that it is also a further element of his obedience as Mediator. He has a commandment—a charge—from the Father to take his life up again. Jesus approaches the cross, not as one would take a risk, but as one would obey a master, knowing that the Father would give him all the help he needed to fulfil his obligations and discharge his duties.

Jesus refers to the resurrection in a striking analogy in John 2. When asked about the temple precincts and the future of the temple, Jesus says, 'Destroy this temple, and in three days I will raise it up' (John 2:19). Not surprisingly, those around him wondered how a temple which was still being repaired after half a century of workmanship could be raised in three days. John continues:

But he was speaking about the temple of his body. When therefore he was raised from the dead, his disciples remembered that he had said this, and they believed the Scripture and the word that Jesus had spoken (John 2:21–22).

All that the temple signified of God's presence with his people was now realized in the incarnate Christ. The unfolding of God's redemptive plan meant that the temple, as part of the Old Testament system, was like scaffolding round a building, which can be taken down once the building is complete. Now, in Christ, God's purposes of salvation, which had focused to such a large extent on the temple in the Old Testament, were fulfilled. Old things were to pass away. All things were to become new. Yet the very analogy showed that here was continuity with all that had gone before. The temple was now to be a spiritual entity, lived in the resurrection power and life of the One who incarnated, in his very life, the Immanuel principle of the temple—God was with his people.

So Jesus anticipates his resurrection as a temple-building, a continuation and further development in the work of God's salvation for a lost world. He looks forward to it, knowing that the body he possesses at that moment will be raised in the power of new and immortal life.

Second, we need to see how *the apostles speak of the resurrection*. In some places they make it clear that the resurrection was particularly the act of God the Father, vindicating the position of Jesus as Saviour and Mediator. Look at the following Scriptures which demonstrate this fact to us:

If we are being examined today concerning a good deed done to a crippled man, by what means this man has been healed, let it be known to all of you and to all the people of Israel that by the name of Jesus Christ of Nazareth, whom you crucified, *whom God raised from the dead*—by him this man is standing before you well (Acts 4:9–10).

Now may the *God of peace who brought again from the dead our Lord Jesus,* the great shepherd of the sheep, by the blood of the eternal covenant, equip you with everything good that you may do his will, working in us that which is pleasing in his sight, through Jesus Christ, to whom be glory for ever and ever (Hebrews 13:20–21).

Both in the statement of Peter following the healing of the crippled man, and in the blessing of Hebrews, the resurrection of Jesus is explicitly stated to be the act of God the Father, loosing Jesus from the bondage of the grave, and giving him glory in the act of resurrection.

Paul adds another slant to this in Romans 1:4, where he says that Jesus, God's Son, was raised by the power of the Holy Spirit. Jesus was

descended from David according to the flesh, and was declared to be the Son of God *in power according to the Spirit of holiness* by his resurrection from the dead.

By the resurrection, God the Father declared Jesus to be his Son in power, through the Holy Spirit. The meaning is not that this was the moment at which Jesus became God's Son. He was always, eternally, unalterably the Son of God. But now the resurrection shows him to be God's Son in a powerful way, possessing a power that was not always evident. Now, with the raising of Jesus, the truth of who he is is potently manifest to all who will believe.

So, Jesus is risen as One who is raised from the dead. His Father, in the audible voice of transfiguration, declared him to be the one in whom he was well pleased. Now he declares the same truth in the silent glory of resurrection. Raising Jesus from the dead was 'the seal that the Father's eternal purpose of love with respect to men had been realized in their redemption through Jesus' blood'.3

So what does this mean for me?

What is the consequence for Christian faith—indeed, for me

Chapter 5

personally—of the doctrine of the resurrection? Or, to put it otherwise, what do I have if I believe and trust in a risen Jesus?

A risen Jesus is a personal Jesus

Sometimes we need to state the obvious. The risen Jesus honoured, loved and proclaimed by the apostles was no figment of their imagination. He was real and he was personal. When he appeared to the disciples,

They were startled and frightened and thought they saw a spirit. And he said to them, 'Why are you troubled, and why do doubts arise in your hearts? See my hands and my feet, that it is I myself. Touch me and see. For a spirit does not have flesh and bones as you see that I have' (Luke 24:37–38).

It was this personal Jesus that the women held by the feet and worshipped (Matthew 28:9). It was this Jesus that Mary Magdalene held on to until Jesus said to her, 'Do not cling to me' (John 20:17). It was this Jesus that ate and drank with the disciples after the resurrection (Acts 10:41).

The resurrection was another stage in the experience of the Jesus who had existed from all eternity, had entered into the human race by virginal conception with the complete absence of human paternity, who had lived and died in the company of men and women. Now he was risen, the same Jesus.

And because that is so, we can all relate to him in a personal way. Perhaps that was one reason for his reluctance to allow Mary to keep holding on to him (John 20:17). Her possession of him was not going to depend on physical nearness, or on a physical relationship. It was going to be realized in a spiritual way. And now, as a result of the resurrection, it is possible for us all to have a real relationship with the Saviour. He is ours, and we are his. In a person-to-person encounter, we can know him whom to know is eternal life.

A risen Jesus is a living Jesus

The most we can say about ourselves is that we are alive, and one day we will die. But Jesus can say, 'I died, and behold I am alive for evermore' (Revelation 1:18). He tasted death for men (Hebrews 2:10), identifying with his people as their sin-bearer and taking their place at Calvary. But, for all that his death on the cross was central and fundamental, he was to save his people by his victory over death, and not simply by his submission to it. That is why Paul labours to argue that Jesus was 'delivered up for our trespasses and raised for our justification' (Romans 4:25). Without being delivered up there could be no resurrection, and without resurrection there could be no justification.

So if it was possible for Job, in the shadows of the Old Testament, to say, 'I know that my Redeemer lives' (Job 19:25), how much more is it possible for us to say that on this side of the epochal events of Calvary and of the open grave? We do not worship Christ for the life he lived once, or even for the death he died once; we worship him for the life that he continues to have and to enjoy.

Paul tells us that the driving power in his life as a preacher and apostle was to know and experience more of that resurrection life in his soul:

… that I may know him and the power of his resurrection, and may share his sufferings, becoming like him in his death, that by any means possible I may attain the resurrection from the dead (Philippians 3:10–11).

Henry Scougal, the Puritan, described religion as 'the life of God in the soul of man'. That is what it means to be a Christian—to have the resurrection life of the Son of God in our souls, so that we are Christians by impulse and by a principle of new life in Christ. We know Jesus as a risen Saviour, not simply personally, but as the one who lives for evermore, formed in us by the Holy Spirit, and interceding for us at God's right hand.

A risen Jesus is a triumphant Jesus

By his resurrection, Jesus stood on the neck of death and of the grave. This was an act of triumph. He has gone up with a shout and with the sound of a trumpet (Psalm 47:5). The cross was not simply the action of a priest, officiating at an altar and offering a sacrifice; it was the action of a king, who was going out to engage in warfare on hostile territory against the enemy of his people. Hebrews 2:14 explicitly states that the action of the cross was focused on the destruction of Satan and the emancipation of his slaves.

Perhaps this is the idea in view when Isaiah describes the Messiah as one would describe the returning army of a conquering hero:

Who is this who comes from Edom, in crimsoned garments from Bozrah, he who is splendid in his apparel, marching in the greatness of his strength? 'It is I, speaking in righteousness, mighty to save.' Why is your apparel red, and your garments like his who treads in the winepress?

I have trodden the winepress alone, and from the peoples no one was with me; I trod them in my anger and trampled them in my wrath; their lifeblood spattered on my garments and stained all my apparel. For the day of vengeance was in my heart and my year of redemption had come (Isaiah 63:1–4).

The language is unmistakably that of war, and the Messiah speaks as one who has effected a great deliverance.

It is in the resurrection of Jesus that we see the fulfilment of this great prophetic vision. Having reached the shores of death, our great conquering King has plundered the very citadels of darkness and, like David on the battlefield, has killed the giant with its own sword. Through death, he destroyed death (Hebrews 2:14), breaking its chains and rendering obsolete its power and claims on those for whom he died.

So, unlike us, Jesus did not live until he had 'one foot in the grave'. He marched into death, facing it with consummate bravery and engaging it with ultimate triumph. He has now marched out of death's dark vaults. By his death, he killed the hostility between us and God (Ephesians 2:16). By his resurrection he has 'abolished death and brought life and immortality to light' (2 Timothy 1:10).

A risen Jesus is a sovereign Jesus

If Jesus is able to conquer death, what will he not conquer? He sits enthroned now in heaven as the one whose pathway to glory has led him to the grave, through the grave, and out of the grave. In our case, all our paths of glory lead to the grave. But in Christ's case, the path of the grave led to glory. And it is as the risen, sovereign Lamb in the midst of heaven's throne that Christ governs his people and guides them to his dwelling-place.

At last, the great issue for us is whether we, like Thomas, can fall down before the risen Christ saying, 'My Lord and my God!' (John 20:28). For, at last, being a Christian means nothing if it does not mean saying 'Jesus is Lord!'

A risen Jesus is a unique Jesus

In this, as in all other aspects of his Mediatorial work, Jesus stands completely and utterly alone. He has no equal; he has no peer. No one comes close to resembling this. The religions of the world honour their leaders, do homage to their memories, respect their tombs. But Jesus is unique. He actually rose from the dead.

Indeed, it was on the basis of the declaration of the raising of Jesus that Peter could assert that 'there is salvation in no one else, for there is no other name under heaven given among men by which we must be saved' (Acts 4:12). In this day of religious plurality and diversity, we must insist on the uniqueness of the risen Christ. In the case of all religious leaders, their death has declared them to be sons of men in weakness. But in this case, Jesus' resurrection declares him to be the Son of God in power.

Among prophets, there is none like Jesus. Among priests, he stands alone. Among kings, he is greater than all. There just is none like him; having conquered death he holds all things in his hand with the promise and guarantee of our victory too:

Since we believe that Jesus died and rose again, even so, through Jesus, God will bring with him those who have fallen asleep (1 Thessalonians 4:14).

Notes

1 **B.B. Warfield,** 'The Resurrection of Christ a historical fact', in J.E. Meeter (ed.) *Selected Shorter Writings of B.B. Warfield,* Vol.I (Nutley, NJ: Presbyterian and Reformed, 1970), p. 178.

2 **T.V. Moore,** *The Last Days of Jesus* (1858, reprinted Edinburgh: The Banner of Truth Trust, 1981), p. 18.

3 **John Murray,** 'Who raised up Jesus?' in *Collected Writings*, Vol. 4 (Edinburgh: The Banner of Truth Trust,) p. 91.

The wonder of Pentecost

This Jesus God raised up, and of that we all are witnesses. Being therefore exalted at the right hand of God, and having received from the Father the promise of the Holy Spirit, he has poured out this that you yourselves are seeing and hearing (Acts 2:32–33).

Anyone who does not have the Spirit of Christ does not belong to him (Romans 8:9).

T he sixth point on which the Bible's story hangs is the wonderful moment when the Holy Spirit fills the disciples on the Day of Pentecost (Acts 2). 'Pentecost' was the feast that was held fifty days after Passover (the word 'pentecost' comes from the Greek word for 'fifty'). The Old Testament regulated it in this way:

You shall count seven full weeks from the day after the Sabbath, from the day that you brought the sheaf of the wave offering. You shall count fifty days to the day after the seventh Sabbath. Then you shall present a grain offering of new grain to the LORD (Leviticus 23:15–16).

The significance of this will be lost on us if we do not realize that the Day of Pentecost always fell on the first day of the week. Thus, although the Old Testament maintained a seventh day of the week Sabbath, the Day of Pentecost was always the day after the seventh Sabbath. This is the time reference in Acts 2:1—the coming of the Day of Pentecost saw the disciples in Jerusalem, waiting, as Christ had commanded them, for the Holy Spirit. Christ ascended into heaven (Acts 1:9) and said to his disciples:

You will receive power when the Holy Spirit has come upon you, and you will be my witnesses in Jerusalem and in all Judea and Samaria, and to the end of the earth (Acts 1:8).

Without any warning, the Holy Spirit came down on the disciples, filled them and enabled them to speak 'in other tongues' (Acts 2:4). It was Peter who defended the disciples against the charge of being drunk. He made three important points about the Holy Spirit to the assembled crowd.

First, Peter highlights that what had happened was *exactly what the Old Testament had anticipated:*

In the last days it shall be, God declares, that I will pour out my Spirit on all flesh, and your sons and your daughters shall prophesy, and your young men shall see visions and your old men shall dream dreams; even on my male servants and female servants in those days I will pour out my Spirit and they shall prophesy (Acts 2:17–18, citing Joel 2:28–29).

Nothing that had taken place ought to have been a surprise. For those who knew their Old Testament, the surprise would have been had the event NOT occurred. Along a line of prophetic vision, Joel is able to see into the future, and to bear witness to the fact that among God's final acts of salvation and redemption would be the outpouring of the Holy Spirit on all flesh. That this promise should arise out of Israel, the nation which God himself had blessed with his covenant salvation in such a unique manner, was itself wonderful. Though confined for so long to one nation, God's salvation was to reach out to the whole world. While much of the external scaffolding of true religion was given to one nation, the Holy Spirit was to be poured out on all.

Second, Peter declares that *the presence of the Holy Spirit is the gift of the ascended Christ.* 'He has poured out this that you yourselves are seeing and hearing' (Acts 2:33). Isaiah had declared of the Messiah that he would sprinkle many nations (52:15), and John the Baptist had promised that Jesus would baptize with the Holy Spirit and with fire (Matthew 3:11).

Indeed, Jesus himself had declared that, for this reason, the disciples would have greater benefit from his leaving them than if he had stayed:

When the Helper comes, whom I will send to you from the Father, the Spirit of truth, who proceeds from the Father, he will bear witness about me. And you also will bear witness, because you have been with me from the beginning (John 15:26–27).

It is to your advantage that I go away, for if I do not go away, the Helper will not come to you. But if I go, I will send him to you (John 16:7).

Now Peter is telling the crowd that these promises, too, have been fulfilled, and that Christ is continuing to exercise a Mediatorial role as the Saviour of his people, pouring out on them the Holy Spirit just as he had said.

Third, Peter says that *those who are listening to him may receive the Holy Spirit too.* Initially, it was the disciples who were filled with the Holy Spirit. But in his address, Peter opened the possibility that others could receive him:

Repent and be baptized every one of you in the name of Jesus Christ for the forgiveness of your sins and you will receive the gift of the Holy Spirit. For the promise is for you and for your children, and for all who are far off, everyone whom the Lord our God calls to himself (Acts 2:38–39).

This promise is what led to about three thousand people trusting in Jesus and receiving the Holy Spirit. Throughout the book of Acts, the same phenomenon occurs. When Saul of Tarsus is brought to his knees after a vision of Christ, Jesus sends Ananias to him, saying,

Brother Saul, the Lord Jesus who appeared to you on the road by which you came has sent me so that you may regain your sight and be filled with the Holy Spirit (Acts 9:17).

In the house of Cornelius, following the preaching of Peter, we read that

The Holy Spirit fell on all who heard the word. And the believers from among the circumcised who had come with Peter were amazed, because the gift of the Holy Spirit was poured out even on the Gentiles (Acts 10:44–45).

When Paul himself became a preacher, he came to Ephesus, where he asked the disciples 'Did you receive the Holy Spirit when you believed?' (Acts 19:3). When they said that they knew nothing about the Holy Spirit, Paul baptized them; we then read that

When Paul had laid his hands on them, the Holy Spirit came on them, and they began speaking in tongues and prophesying (Acts 19:6).

So the same Holy Spirit who fell on the believers at Pentecost was also experienced by others; moreover, one of the consequences of the phenomenon was that those who received the Spirit were able to speak in other languages and to 'prophesy'.

What about today?

One would think that in view of these things, the doctrine of the Holy Spirit would be straightforward. But in the church there have been many controversies surrounding the doctrine of the Holy Spirit. Should we, today, be speaking in tongues? Should we be experiencing another Pentecost? What does it mean for us that we are living in this age of the Holy Spirit?

As we look at these and other questions, let's bear in mind that we are living in the 'last days', the days in which God said he would pour out his Spirit on all flesh, the days in which the Holy Spirit as the great Helper of his people, enables the work of the kingdom to progress, and ensures that the work of the gospel will be prosperous. This is what everything God did in the Old Testament through Israel, and climactically in the New Testament through Jesus Christ, is for. Consider again these great words of Paul:

Christ redeemed us from the curse of the law by becoming a curse for us—for it is written, 'Cursed is everyone who is hanged on a tree'—so that in Christ Jesus the blessing of Abraham might come to the Gentiles, *so that we might receive the promised Spirit through faith*. (Galatians 3:13–14).

It is important for us to grasp that today God is with us in this great wonder of Pentecost; and 'through the Spirit, by faith, we ourselves eagerly wait for the hope of righteousness' (Galatians 5:5).

Who is the Holy Spirit?

In the Old Testament, the idea of God's spirit is largely equated with God's power at work, his divine activity. So when we read that 'the Spirit of God was hovering over the face of the waters' (Genesis 1:2) we are going to hear of God's sovereign power in creation. Similarly, in Micah 3:8 the prophet says, 'I am filled with power, with the Spirit of the LORD, and with justice and might, to declare to Jacob his transgression and to Israel his sin'. The ministry of the prophet, as the work of creation, is by the power and activity of God.

If, therefore, we were to confine ourselves to the Old Testament, we might conclude that God is a singular person, and that the references to the power and spirit of the Lord are references to God's might and greatness and authority. Yet, while the references to God's spirit are no less than this, with the unfolding of biblical revelation we discover much more.

Sinclair Ferguson[1] suggests that we need to break down the question about the identity of the Holy Spirit into three questions. First: 'Is the activity of the Spirit *divine* activity?' The answer is an obvious 'yes'. Second: 'Is the activity of the Spirit *personal* activity?' Again, the answer is 'yes'. Third: 'Is the activity of the Spirit hypostatically [personally] distinct?'[2] That is, can it be distinguished from the activity of God the Father and God the Son?

This last question is crucial, and involves a recognition of the difference between the Old Testament and the New. It is with the coming of Christ that the nature of God is more fully revealed to us. Indeed, Christ declares it to be his function, as the God who is only-begotten, to reveal to us the God that no one has ever seen (John 1:18). By knowing God we can have eternal life (John 17:3). In the same way, Jesus reveals the Holy Spirit to us (a ministry paralleled in the fact that the Holy Spirit reveals Jesus to us). It was to be with the glorifying of Christ that the Spirit was to be given (John 7:39); and the Spirit is both the Spirit of Christ (Romans 8:9) and the Spirit who proceeds from the Father (John 15:26).

So, with the coming of Jesus, we appreciate something that was to a large extent concealed, yet not altogether hidden, in the Old Testament: that God is, in fact, three Persons: Father, Son and Holy Spirit. This is brought out clearly in the baptism formula of Matthew 28:19–20:

Go therefore and make disciples of all nations, baptizing them in the name [singular] of the Father and of the Son and of the Holy Spirit, teaching them to observe all that I have commanded you. And behold, I am with you always, to the end of the age.

In the light of Scripture, we cannot think of the Holy Spirit as an impersonal force or simply a mysterious power at work among men. We must think of him as we think of the Father and of the Son: God, in person, at work in the world. It is precisely because that is so that we can now know God:

What no eye has seen, nor ear heard, nor the heart of man imagined, what God has prepared for those who love him—these things God has revealed to us through the Spirit. For the Spirit searches everything, even the depths of God ... Now we have received not the spirit of the world, but the Spirit who is from God, that we might understand the things freely given us by God (1 Corinthians 2:9–12).

What did the Holy Spirit do in the past?

It is a mistake, therefore, to imagine that the Holy Spirit only appeared at Pentecost, as if he was missing from God's work in the world before then. There are several points we need to bear in mind.

First, *the Holy Spirit enabled God's people to fulfil the duties, task and service that were allotted to them.* Of the judges, for example, we read that the Spirit came upon Othniel (Judges 3:10), Gideon (6:34), Jephthah (11:29) and Samson (14:19). In connection with David's anointing to be king, we also read that the Spirit of the Lord came upon him (1 Samuel 16:13). The ultimate Old Testament hope was for the Messiah to come, who would also be given the Holy Spirit (Isaiah 61:1).

Although we cannot say that the Old Testament saints did not have the Holy Spirit, we do need to appreciate the difference in the way the Bible speaks about the Holy Spirit in the Testaments. The emphasis in the Old Testament is on empowerment: the Spirit *coming upon* an individual. The emphasis in the New Testament is on indwelling: the Spirit *dwelling* in an individual.

Second, *the Holy Spirit in the Old Testament was particularly a spirit of prophecy.* As Peter reminds us:

Concerning this salvation, the prophets who prophesied about the grace that was to be yours searched and enquired carefully, enquiring what person or time the Spirit of Christ in them was indicating when he predicted the sufferings of Christ and the subsequent glories. It was revealed to them that they were serving not themselves but you, in the things that have now been announced to you through those who preached the good news to you by the Holy Spirit sent from heaven, things into which angels long to look (1 Peter 1:10–12).

The spirit of prophecy was the Spirit of Christ, active in the Old Testament among those whose calling it was to point men towards the coming Messiah. And it is precisely in connection with this that Peter can argue for the inspiration and inerrancy of the Old Testament Scriptures:

No prophecy of Scripture comes from someone's own interpretation. For no prophecy was ever produced by the will of man, but men spoke from God as they were carried along by the Holy Spirit (2 Peter 1:20–21).

Third, *the Holy Spirit ministered in a remarkable way to the person of Jesus Christ*. Jesus' body was conceived through the power of the Holy Spirit. He was filled with the Spirit for the public ministry in which he was to engage. He was led by that Spirit into various situations, including the time of testing in the wilderness. He was enabled to offer himself to God through the Holy Spirit. Of Jesus alone can it be said that the Holy Spirit was not given to him with any limitation or measurement.

What does the Holy Spirit do now?

First, *the Holy Spirit gives us spiritual life*: 'It is the Spirit who gives life; the flesh is no help at all' (John 6:63). This is what Octavius Winslow, in his old but excellent work on the Holy Spirit, describes as 'the Spirit's first gracious and Divine act—the breathing of spiritual life in the soul … The Spirit's work as a Quickener must ever precede his work as a Sanctifier and a Comforter'.[3]

Paul reminds us that without Christ, we are dead in trespasses and sins (Ephesians 2:1). To be without Christ is to be separated from God, and that is to be in a state of death. But the Holy Spirit is the one who brings dead souls alive. If we do not have the Spirit of Christ, we remain in our dead state, and we cannot belong to Christ (see Romans 8:9). But to be 'born of the Spirit' (John 3:6, 8) is to have Christ, as Paul explains:

If Christ is in you, although the body is dead because of sin, the Spirit is life because of righteousness. If the Spirit of him who raised Jesus from the dead dwells in you, he who raised Christ Jesus from the dead will also give life to your mortal bodies through his Spirit who dwells in you (Romans 8:10–11).

In this passage, the future resurrection is the logical extension of the Spirit-life which has already come to be imparted to our souls. To have the Spirit is to have Christ as Saviour. To have Christ as Saviour is to be born of the Spirit. Or, as the New Testament puts it: 'Now the Lord is the Spirit, and where the Spirit of the Lord is, there is freedom' (2 Corinthians 3:17).

The New Testament knows nothing of having Christ but not having the Spirit. When the disciples received the Spirit at Pentecost it was not in order to show us that receiving the Holy Spirit is an experience subsequent to conversion. Pentecost was a unique and definitive event marking the beginning of the Holy Spirit's public, Christ-honouring ministry in the world. Those who have Christ have the Spirit, and they are called to live by the Spirit.

Interestingly, what took place at Pentecost immediately led to Peter preaching, not about the Holy Spirit, but about Jesus Christ. The sign of the presence of the Spirit was a Christ-centred and Christ-exalting proclamation. This, too, fulfilled what Jesus said:

When the Spirit of truth comes, he will guide you into all the truth, for he will not speak on his own authority, but whatever he hears he will speak, and he will declare to you the things that are to come. He will glorify me, for he will take what is mine and declare it to you (John 16:13–14).

The ministry of the Spirit is to exalt Jesus. When a soul becomes spiritually alive, Jesus is loved, honoured and obeyed. When the gospel is preached in the power of the Spirit, Christ and his saving work are proclaimed, exalted and magnified before people. When a church is revived in the power of the Spirit, Christ becomes the object of love, affection and service. The mark of the Holy Spirit's presence in lives, pulpits and congregations is that in all things, as a result, Christ has the pre-eminence (Colossians 1:18), as the one in whom all the fullness of God dwells (1:19).

Second, *the Holy Spirit indwells us.* The principle is laid down in 1 Corinthians 6:19: 'your body is a temple of the Holy Spirit'. Just as the glory of God dwelt in Solomon's temple, so the Holy Spirit has residence in the life of God's child. In context, Paul is urging the Corinthian believers to make sure that their bodies are consecrated to Christ. The reason he gives is astounding: it is because the Spirit is dwelling there. As Octavius Winslow puts it:

Through the incarnation, obedience, death and resurrection of Christ, a way was opened by which God could again dwell with man, could resume his abode in the very temple that sin had destroyed, and show forth the riches and glory of his grace far more illustriously than when this temple stood in its original perfection and grandeur.[4]

This was nothing other than what the prophets had foretold. Ezekiel prophesied of a day when God would put his Spirit within his people (Ezekiel 36:27; 37:14). Of this Spirit, Jesus said that he would be in us (John 14:17), and that the Spirit would be like rivers of water flowing out of our heart (John 7:38, probably referring to the vision of a river of water pouring out of the temple in Ezekiel 47). Paul, too, declares that 'the Spirit of God dwells in you' (Romans 8:9).

If this is so, then there is no part of the Christian that does not belong to Christ. We are no longer our own. Our lives are Spirit-possessed, or else they cannot be Spirit-led and Christ-honouring.

Third, *the Holy Spirit sanctifies us.* The Holy Spirit, by definition, is the spirit of holiness (Romans 1:4). He effects what Christ secured by his dying: that a people would be holy, freed from sin and committed to the honour and glory of God. Or, as George Smeaton puts it, 'There cannot be the application of redemption in the way of pardon and acceptance without the accompanying spirit of holiness'.[5]

To *sanctify* something is to set it apart for God's glory and use. Believers in Christ are *saints* (see, for example, 1 Corinthians 1:2). By giving us the Holy Spirit, the risen Christ sets us apart, makes us holy people, and sets us on the way to heaven which is a way of holiness (Isaiah 35:8). But the Holy Spirit then sanctifies us *progressively*, step by step and stage by stage. To use the terminology of the Westminster Shorter Catechism, sanctification is a work, not an act. Paul puts it this way:

We all, with unveiled face, beholding the glory of the Lord, are being transformed into the same image from one degree of glory to another. For this comes from the Lord who is the Spirit (2 Corinthians 3:18).

The purpose of the Spirit is to enable us to live Christ-like lives, so that our attention will be focused on Jesus. Another way of saying this is that the Holy Spirit works to produce a certain kind of character in us, identified as the 'fruit of the Spirit' in Galatians 5:22–24:

The fruit of the Spirit is love, joy, peace, patience, kindness, goodness, faithfulness, gentleness, self-control; against such things there is no law. And those who belong to Christ Jesus have crucified the flesh with its passions and desires.

There is, therefore, a difference between the gifts of the Spirit, such as tongue-speaking and miracles, which were evident at Pentecost, and which were only given to a few believers in the early church, and the fruit of the Spirit, which must be the lifestyle of all God's children. There is a struggle going on between the Spirit and the 'flesh' (Galatians 5:17; cf. Romans 7:21–25), which means that we can never attain to perfection in this life. But we are to keep our minds on the Spirit and follow him, for 'all who are led by the Spirit of God are sons of God' (Romans 8:14).

As part of this sanctifying ministry, the Holy Spirit enables us to obey God's law with a delight and willingness. By redeeming us from the law's curse, God enables us to meet the law's demands:

By sending his own Son in the likeness of sinful flesh and for sin, he condemned sin in the flesh, in order that the righteous requirement of the law might be fulfilled in us, who walk not according to the flesh but according to the Spirit (Romans 8:3–4).

The age of the Holy Spirit is not a lawless age. In fact, the same covenant promise that said that the Spirit would be within us also said that God's law would be written on our hearts (Jeremiah 31:33). It is an age in which

God's people can say, 'Oh how I love your law! It is my meditation all the day' (Psalm 119:97). Just like Israel in the Old Testament, we have been redeemed to serve God. We have not been saved *from* law-keeping, but *to* law-keeping. We are not saved by our obedience, but we show our salvation and our faith in our obedience, and live the way God wants us to live.

So when Peter talks about the work of the triune God in our salvation, he talks of 'the foreknowledge of God the Father, in the sanctification of the Spirit, for obedience to Jesus Christ …' (1 Peter 1:2). Just as the Father's election and the Son's obedience are essential to our salvation, so the Spirit's sanctifying, cleansing work is every bit as essential.

Fourth, *the Holy Spirit seals us*. There is a reference to this at Ephesians 1:13–14.

In him you also, when you heard the word of truth, the gospel of your salvation, and believed in him, were sealed with the promised Holy Spirit, who is the guarantee of our inheritance until we acquire possession of it, to the praise of his glory.

Whatever we understand this sealing of the Spirit to be, it is clear that it is the characteristic of those who trust in Jesus, and it is necessary because we have not yet entered into the full possession of our inheritance in Jesus Christ. We are living in the interim between redemption and realization— saved by his grace, and pressing onward to glory.

What if we should stumble along the way? Is there any danger of us not making it? Well, that is precisely the point here—the King has set his seal on us, making his ownership of us plain, and pledging to keep us safe and protect us until we reach the end of the journey.

There has been much discussion in theology over whether this seal is something subsequent to conversion, or whether it is identified with it. Paul seems to assume later in the epistle that all believers are sealed, when he says, 'do not grieve the Holy Spirit of God, by whom you were sealed for the day of redemption' (Ephesians 4:30). Their being sealed does not mean that they will not sin; it is possible for them to grieve the God by whom their salvation is made secure. Yet the fact that that is so suggests that God has no children whom he has not sealed, and that all enjoy the blessing and the privilege of being kept safe and secure until the day of redemption comes.

To what extent is this seal a conscious experience in the life of the believer? The older Puritan view seems to be that by the Spirit's sealing was meant an assurance of our salvation and our sonship. This is how Octavius Winslow understood it:

In most cases the sealing of the Spirit is a more gradual work. It is a work of time. The soul is placed in the school of deep experience and is led on step by step, stage by stage. The knowledge of self and of Christ increases, deeper views of indwelling sin are discovered, the heart's treachery is more acutely felt, the devices of Satan are better known, the mystery of God's gracious and providential dealings with his children is more clearly unfolded and better understood. And all this, it may be, is arrived at through a process, the deep, painful yet sanctified discipline of the covenant, so that years may elapse before a child of the covenant attains to the full sealing of the Spirit.[6]

It seems to me that although Winslow may be describing a genuine aspect of the Christian life, he is not describing a seal, which, by its very nature, is made once, in order to be a permanent mark. Its function is external to the believer—it is what identifies the Christian as being under the authority and protection of the King. To that extent, I think Winslow is describing something other than the sealing of the Spirit, although he is certainly describing something relating to it.

Fifth, *the Holy Spirit witnesses in us*. The classic text is Romans 8:16–17:

The Spirit himself bears witness with our spirit that we are children of God, and if children, then heirs—heirs of God and fellow heirs with Christ, provided we suffer with him in order that we may also be glorified with him.

What is this saying to us? It is saying that it is our privilege to know about our freedom and salvation in Jesus Christ. It belongs to the ministry of the Holy Spirit to bring the impression to bear on our hearts and minds that all that the Bible says about a Christian it is saying about us personally.

There is, therefore, a correlation between the witness of the Spirit in the heart and the witness of the Spirit in the Bible. The Bible is a Spirit-inspired book; the Christian is a Spirit-led person. By opening eyes to the grandeur of the Bible's teaching, the Holy Spirit opens the eyes of the Christian to understand that he or she stands in a unique relation to God in Christ in which all that God has prepared for his people the Christian stands to inherit.

In fact, Paul's reference to the witness of the Holy Spirit is particularly related to the Christian's *sonship*. He has just said that 'you did not receive the spirit of slavery to fall back into fear, but you have received the Spirit of adoption as sons, by whom we cry, "Abba! Father!"' (Romans 8:15). So this witness is really the realization that the relationship we have with God is that of a son to a Father. And as we give expression to these desires, requests and needs, praying in and with the dependence of children, so the Holy Spirit conveys to us more and more that we belong to the family of God.

The apostle John labours this point:

By this we know that we abide in him and he in us, because he has given us of his Spirit (1 John 4:13).

The Spirit is the one who testifies, because the Spirit is the truth … Whoever believes in the Son of God has the testimony in himself (1 John 5:6, 10).

This is the great privilege of God's children. They know who they are, and what they are. By a personal, living, testifying work, they are assured of their standing in Christ. And it is of the nature of that witness that Christ becomes the more precious to them.

Sixth, *the Holy Spirit helps us*. He is the Helper, the Comforter, who draws alongside and stands with God's people in all their situations. He helps them to pray, because they do not know what to pray for as they should (Romans 8:26). Prayer is 'the breathing of the life of God in the soul',7 and is the sure mark that we are Spirit-led.

But if we have neglected to pray, then how can we have the Spirit? And if we do not have the Spirit, we do not belong to Christ. Winslow presses the point—we must do business with God:

Behold, then, the throne of grace! Was ever spot so verdant and so sunny? Was ever resting-place so sacred and so sweet? Could God himself invest it with a richer or greater attraction? Behold it yet again. It is the throne of grace … There sits the God of grace … There is extended the sceptre of grace … There stands Jesus the High-priest and Mediator, full of grace and truth … And there, too, is the Spirit of grace, breathing in the soul, making known the want, putting the petition into words, and making intercession for the saints according to the will of God.[8]

And the Holy Spirit helper is to be with us continually, even to the end of the age (Matthew 28:20). These are the last days. Perhaps in our confusion over who the Holy Spirit is and what the Spirit does, we need to recover these simple basic truths. Where the Spirit is at work, there is a consciousness of God, a desire for holiness, a growth in our assurance, a burden for prayer.

We cannot have Pentecost again. But we can keep on being filled by the Spirit, so that as individuals and as churches, the life and power and pulse of God might flow through us in grace. For it still remains true that it is those who are led by God's Spirit that are God's children (Romans 8:14).

Notes

1 **Sinclair Ferguson,** *The Holy Spirit* (Leicester: IVP, 1998).

2 Ibid. p. 28.

3 **O. Winslow,** *The Work of the Holy Spirit*, (1840, reprinted London: The Banner of Truth Trust, 1961), p. 31. The six main points of this section follow Winslow's outline.

4 Ibid. p. 95.

5 **George Smeaton,** *The Doctrine of the Holy Spirit* (1882, reprinted London: The Banner of Truth Trust, 1958), p. 222.

6 **Winslow,** pp. 140-141.

7 Ibid. p. 199.

8 Ibid. pp. 202–3.

The wonder of Christ's glorious appearing

The Lord himself will descend from heaven (1 Thessalonians 4:16).

We are waiting (2 Peter 3:13).

Our last study is the wonder of the glorious return and second coming of the Lord Jesus Christ. According to the apostle Peter, we have been born again 'to a living hope' (1 Peter 1:3), and, by its very nature, hope looks forward. Christian hope is intimately related to faith and the work of the Holy Spirit (see Romans 5:1–5). All those who trust in Christ can look forward with a sure and certain knowledge of what the future is going to bring, in spite of the fact that there are many things about the future that we cannot know.

In his *Systematic Theology*, Charles Hodge begins his discussion of the second coming of Jesus Christ with a reminder of how limited our knowledge is. He draws our attention to the fact that, even with the benefit of four thousand years of Old Testament history, prophecy and revelation, people still did not understand what Messiah was going to be or do. For example, although many knew he was to be a king, they still failed to realize that his kingdom would not be of this world. Applying this to our interpretation of the prophecy of the New Testament regarding the future, Hodge says to us that

The utter failure of the Old Testament Church in interpreting the prophecies relating to the first advent of Christ should teach us to be modest and diffident in explaining those which relate to his second coming.[1]

In other words, even when we have read and digested the great prophetic insights into the glorious appearing of Jesus, it still remains true that the appearing of Jesus will surpass our highest conceptions of it. Perhaps, indeed, we will realize that we were only skimming the surface.

Nevertheless, there is a great amount of material in the New Testament concerning this theme, a theme that reminds us that history has a purpose and a goal. It is not going to drift on for ever; God will bring his world to an ordered and precise termination. To use Peter's language, all things will continue as they have been from the beginning of creation (see 2 Peter 3:4) until 'the day of the Lord' (2 Peter 3:10) comes. That, says Peter, is what we are awaiting: the moment when the Lord himself will descend from heaven.

So, although there are many things which we do not know, there are other things of which we can be certain. And no wonder: a great deal of the Bible is occupied with this theme. James Montgomery Boice, for example, makes the following observations:

In the New Testament, one verse in twenty-five deals with the Lord's return. It is mentioned 318 times in the 260 chapters … The return of Jesus Christ is mentioned in every one of the New Testament books except Galatians (which was written with a particular and quite different problem in view) and the very short books such as 2 and 3 John and Philemon. Jesus spoke of his return quite often.[2]

We know WHO is going to return: 'The Lord himself'

When Christ ascended to heaven, the angels bore witness that 'this Jesus, who was taken up from you into heaven, will come in the same way as you saw him go into heaven' (Acts 1:11). Thus the New Testament identifies the coming Christ, who is going to come in splendour and majesty, with the Christ who came first in humility, lowliness and dishonour.

His angels will appear, and tens of thousands of his saints will appear: but the great hope of the church is that Jesus himself will appear. No one will deputize for him. He will not send an ambassador. He will be revealed in the glory of his majesty as the King that he is.

The reason for this is simple: it is to the Christ who died at Calvary that the Father has given a name above every name, at which every knee will bow and confess his Lordship (Philippians 2:8–11). The second coming is nothing other than the consummation of the covenant promises, and the vindication of the honour of God in the salvation of his people.

We know something about HOW he is going to return

1 Thessalonians 4 tells us that Christ's return will be *visible*. Jesus will descend from 'heaven'. This follows a biblical motif which is very important. In the Old Testament tabernacle, a special curtain marked off the place where God's glory and presence resided among his people. Only the high priest could enter there, once a year. The veil represented the great distance between God and men. At the beginning of his ministry, with his baptism, Mark tells us Jesus saw the heavens opening and the Spirit descending on him like a dove (Mark 1:10). The word for 'opening' there is really 'being torn apart'. With the ministry of Jesus, heaven was pressing in on earth, as the only-begotten God in the bosom of the Father came to reveal God to men. When he died, that temple veil was torn (Mark 15:38), and the way to God was opened.

The gospel is all about Christ having made access to God for us. And ultimately, when Jesus returns, it will be in his glory, with the angels (Matthew 25:31), with the last veil taken away, and we shall be face to face with God. We will see him as he is.

In other words, it will be a public event, and it will be incontrovertible. No one will be able to persuade anyone that the return is not really the return. As John Murray puts it, 'When Christ comes there can be no deception because there will be no concealment'.[3] It will be a revelation, an unveiling, a *parousia*, a presence.

His return will also be *audible*. It will not be silent and secret, like the resurrection. Jesus will come with the fanfare of the angels, with the trumpet sound of God and the voice of the archangel (1 Thessalonians 4:16). There will be an arresting quality to his return. The noise will drown out all other noises. The voice will stop all other conversations. The trumpet will stop all other singing and music. The heavens will pass away with a roar (2 Peter 3:10). Above the din of this present evil world there will be the majestic heralding of the coming King.

His return will be *climactic*. In the words of Peter, 'the earth and the works that are done on it will be exposed [or burned up] … the heavens will be set on fire and dissolved, and the heavenly bodies will melt as they burn! (2 Peter 3:10–12). This is captured powerfully by John in Revelation 6:12ff:

When he opened the sixth seal, I looked, and behold, there was a great earthquake, and the sun became black as sackcloth, the full moon became like blood, and the stars of the sky fell to the earth as the fig tree sheds its winter fruit when shaken by a gale. The sky vanished like a scroll that is being rolled up, and every mountain and island was removed from its place. Then the kings of the earth and the great ones and the generals and the rich and the powerful, and everyone, slave and free, hid themselves in the caves and among the rocks of the mountains, calling to the mountains and rocks, 'Fall on us and hide us from the face of him who is seated on the throne, and from the wrath of the Lamb, for the great day of their wrath has come, and who can stand?'

Christ himself compares the second coming to the flood, which swept away the old order, renewing the earth for his covenant people. Perhaps that is a sign that the new heavens and the new earth are to be a renewed universe, fit for a renewed people. But whatever is the case, the present order will come to its end, and the coming of Jesus will mark that end.

We may imagine that this is a terrible thing. But the creation itself is longing for the moment when it will be 'set free from its bondage to corruption and obtain the freedom of the glory of the children of God' (Romans 8:21). Creation is groaning in pains, the pangs, as John Murray puts it, of birth, not of death.[4] The result will be a created order as it was always meant to be.

We know WHY he is going to return

First, he is returning *to display his glory*. In his first advent, that glory was hidden; during this period of the gospel, his glory is despised. Few bow the knee or acknowledge his lordship. And although there is a strand of gospel teaching that suggests that there will be success and blessing for the gospel in these last days in which we live, there is another strand which teaches that things will get worse and worse. That is what Paul declares to Timothy:

But understand this, that in the last days there will come times of difficulty. For people will be lovers of self, lovers of money, proud, arrogant, abusive, disobedient to their parents, ungrateful, unholy, heartless, unappeasable, slanderous, without self-control, brutal, not loving good, treacherous, reckless, swollen with conceit, lovers of pleasure rather than lovers of God, having the appearance of godliness, but denying its power (2 Timothy 3:1–5).

Or, as Peter puts it, 'scoffers will come in the last days' (2 Peter 3:3). This is not an age that acknowledges the glory of Jesus. But these lying, scoffing, rebellious lips will one day acknowledge that glory does indeed belong to the Lord. The proud man will eat his words. The rebellious man will fall silent before the awesome majesty of Jesus. The man who lives for his own glory will come to realize that glory belongs to Jesus Christ.

Second, Christ will come *to raise his people from their graves*. That is Paul's teaching in 1 Thessalonians, with its practical purpose of giving comfort and encouragement to those who imagined that their beloved Christian dead would somehow miss out when Christ comes again. But far from missing out, Paul tells them that 'the dead in Christ will rise first' (1 Thessalonians 4:16). Death will not hold God's people for ever. The coming of Christ will mean their ultimate release from the sleep of death. There will be a resurrection of the dead.

Jesus reminds us that this will be a general resurrection: 'An hour is coming, and is now here, when the dead will hear the voice of the Son of God … all who are in the tombs will hear his voice and come out, those who have done good to the resurrection of life, and those who have done evil to the resurrection of judgement' (John 5:25–29).

Third, Christ will come *to gather together his church*. In this world it is scattered and thrown asunder to the four winds of heaven. Here, the church is spread over many generations and over many places. But it is Christ's design to have his church with him where he is, which is why he promises that 'I will come again and will take you to myself, that where I am you may be also' (John 14:3). Or, to use the words of Christ in Matthew 24:30–31:

Then will appear in heaven the sign of the Son of Man, and then all the tribes of the earth will mourn, and they will see the Son of Man coming on the clouds of heaven with power and great glory. And he will send out his angels with a loud trumpet call, and they will gather his elect from the four winds, from one end of heaven to the other.

The time of separation is over. Christ will come to bring his people, his family, his flock, together. Where will we be when he does that?

Fourth, Christ is coming again *to judge the living and the dead.* His throne, which for us now is described as a throne of grace (Hebrews 4:16) will become a throne of judgement. In Revelation we see the great assembly of men, women and children, before the throne of God and the Lamb. Books are opened; testimonies are given; lives are weighed in the balances of God's law and righteousness. And on the basis of that perfect judgement, there will be a perfect, final and irrevocable verdict—we will either be openly acknowledged and acquitted and made perfectly blessed in the full enjoying of God to all eternity (Shorter Catechism Question 38), or else we will be banished from the presence of the Lord into the hell he has prepared for the devil and his angels.

The only point which we do not know is WHEN he will return

We know that there are events to precede his coming. He will not return until the gospel has been preached all over the world, and until false prophets have done their work, culminating in the appearance of the man of sin or lawlessness (see 2 Thessalonians 2). Some interpret Romans 9–11 to mean that there will also be a great conversion among the Jewish people before Jesus comes again.

But the major emphasis of the New Testament is on one simple fact: his coming will be unexpected. The coming of the Son of Man will be as unexpected as Noah's flood was to his generation. It will be like a thief in the night (2 Peter 3:10).

In the light of this, Jesus has one all-important message to deliver to us: 'Therefore you also must be ready, for the Son of Man is coming at an hour you do not expect' (Matthew 24:44). Are we ready? Would we be ready if he came right now? Are we watching and praying? Have we oil in our lamps lest the cry go out at midnight, saying, 'Here is the bridegroom'? (Matthew 25:6). Are we good and faithful servants, ready for the return of the Master from his long journey? Are we waiting for new heavens and a new earth in which righteousness dwells (2 Peter 3:13)?

Consider the incomparable Jonathan Edwards as he draws these strands of biblical truth together:

Christ will appear in the glory of his Father, with all his holy angels, coming in the clouds of heaven. When the world is thus revelling in their wickedness, and compassing the holy city, just ready to destroy it, then shall the glorious Redeemer make his appearance. He through whom this redemption has all along been carried on, shall appear in the sight of the world; the light of his glory shall break forth; the whole world shall immediately have notice of it, and they shall lift up their eyes and behold this wonderful sight. *Every eye shall see him,* Rev. 1:7.—Christ shall appear coming in his human nature, in that same body (now glorified) which was brought forth in a stable, and laid in a manger, which afterwards was so cruelly used, and nailed to the cross.

Men shall now lift up their eyes, and see him coming in such majesty and glory as now is to us utterly inconceivable. The glory of the sun in a clear firmament will be but darkness in comparison of it; and all the glorious angels and archangels shall attend him, thousand thousands ministering to him, and ten thousand times ten thousand round about him.—How different a person will he then appear from what he did at his first coming, when he was as a root out of a dry ground, a poor, despised, afflicted man! How different now is his appearance, in the midst of those glorious angels, principalities, and powers, in heavenly places, attending him as his ordinary servants, from what it was when in the midst of a ring of soldiers, with his mock robe and his crown of thorns, to be buffeted and spit upon, or hanging on the cross between two thieves, with a multitude of his enemies triumphing over him!

This will be a most unexpected sight to the wicked world; it will come as a cry at midnight. They shall be taken in the midst of their wickedness, and it will give them a dreadful alarm. It will at once break up their revels, their eating, and drinking, and carousing. It will put a quick end to the design of the great army that will then be compassing the camp of the saints; it will make them let drop their weapons out of their hands. The world, which will then be very full of people, most of whom will be wicked men, will then be filled with dolorous shrieking and crying; for all the kindreds of the earth shall wail because of him, Rev. i. 7. And, where shall they hide themselves? How will the sight of that awful majesty terrify them when taken in the midst of their wickedness! Then they shall see who he is, what kind of a person he is, whom they have mocked and scoffed at, and whose church they have been endeavouring to overthrow. This sight will change their voice. The voice of their laughter and singing, while they are marrying and giving in marriage, and the voice of their scoffing, shall be changed into hideous, yea hellish yelling. Their countenances shall be changed from a show of carnal mirth, haughty pride, and contempt of God's people; they shall put on ghastly terror and amazement; and trembling and chattering of teeth shall seize upon them.

But with respect to the saints, it shall be a joyful and most glorious sight to them: for this sight will at once deliver them from all fear of their enemies, who were before compassing them about, just ready to swallow them up. Deliverance shall come in their extremity: the glorious Captain of their salvation shall appear for them, at a time when no other help appeared. Then shall they lift up their heads, and their redemption shall be drawing nigh, (Luke 21:28.) Christ will appear with infinite majesty, yet at the same time they shall see infinite love in his countenance. And thus to see their Redeemer coming in the clouds of heaven, will fill their hearts full of gladness. Their countenances also shall be changed, but not as the countenances of the wicked, but from being sorrowful, to be exceedingly joyful and triumphant. And now the work of redemption will be finished in another sense, *viz.* that the whole church shall be completely and eternally freed from all persecution and molestation from wicked men and devils.[5]

So, as Jesus says to us on the pages of the New Testament, 'Surely I am coming soon', can we respond with John: 'Come, Lord Jesus!' (Revelation 22:20)?

Notes

1 **C. Hodge,** *Systematic Theology*, Volume 3 (Repinted Grand Rapids, MI: Eeerdmans, 1997), p.791.

2 **J.M. Boice,** *Foundations of the Christian Faith* (Leicester: IVP, 1986), pp. 705–706.

3 **John Murray,** *Collected Writings,* Vol 2, (Edinburgh: The Banner of Truth Trust, 1977), p. 404.

4 **John Murray,** *The Epistle to the Romans,* The New International Commentary on the New Testament (Grand Rapids: Eerdmans, 1968), p. 305.

5 **Jonathan Edwards,** 'History of the Work of Redemption' in *Works,* I (reprinted Edinburgh: The Banner of Truth Trust, 1974), p. 612.

What now?

The time is fulfilled, and the kingdom of God is at hand; repent and believe in the gospel (Mark 1:15).

Then he brought them out and said, 'Sirs, what must I do to be saved?' And they said, 'Believe in the Lord Jesus, and you will be saved, you and your household' (Acts 16:30–31)

The storyline of the Bible takes us from absolute beginnings to ultimate conclusions, from the beginning of the world to its consummation and goal. It tells us of the God who made us, and against whom we sinned. It tells the story of his grace, as he stepped in to deliver us from sin and from ourselves. Ultimately, it tells the story of Jesus, in whom alone we can be saved and find the way to God.

Perhaps, having read the story, you are wondering what to do next. The Book of Acts tells the story of a prison warder who reached a crisis point in his life, and was at the point of committing suicide when Paul shouted to him not to harm himself. The events of his life closed him in to the realization that without God he was lost. Paul and Silas, his prisoners, were really free, while he, a free man, was really a slave to sin.

He asked the most important question in the world: '*What must I do to be saved?*' Perhaps you are asking that question now. There is no more vital issue with which to wrestle than this one. Unless we are right with God, nothing in our lives will be right. If we know that we are at peace with him, then we know that our lives are secure. The answer to the question reveals three things:

Only one Saviour

The story of the Bible focuses on one unique person: Jesus Christ. It is to him the apostles turn the heart and attention of the prison warder. 'Believe in *the Lord Jesus*, and you will be saved …' The prophets spoke about him. The psalms spoke about him. The gospels and the letters of the New

Testament spoke about him. Men and women still speak about him. Jesus is the Way to God.

It is possible for us to have a relationship with God through his Son. On his own authority we can say that if we have seen Jesus, we have seen the Father (John 14:9). If we have him, we are complete (Colossians 2:9). And if we are in his hands, no one can threaten our security and eternal salvation (cf. John 10:28, Romans 8:35). That salvation is bound up uniquely with the Person and Work of Jesus. His face appears on the blueprint of the Bible narrative.

Only one salvation

Because there is only one Saviour, there is only one way in which we can be saved. It's not by doing our best, or by living a religious life; not by our own efforts or the works of our own hands. Time and again the Bible story has taught us that God alone must save; that all our best deeds are stained and spotted in the face of his perfect righteousness and holiness.

But that does not mean there is no salvation for us. The gospel comes with good news, and that news calls us to '*Believe* in the Lord Jesus'. That doesn't just mean believing that what the Bible says about him is true—that is, giving mental and intellectual assent to the truth-claims of Scripture. It means more than that.

It means *knowing about* Jesus—that is, knowing that he is the Saviour the Bible declares him to be, and able to do what the Bible says he can do. Our salvation does depend on accepting the facts of the Bible, and assenting to them.

But it means more: it means *believing that he can actually save us*. If I am to experience the salvation Jesus offers, I must believe in his ability and capacity to meet all my needs, to deal with all my sins, to forgive all my past, and to give me all the hope I need for the future. It means believing the truth of the promise that Jesus himself gives us: 'Whoever comes to me I will never cast out' (John 6:37).

But, ultimately, faith means *trusting that Jesus will save me if I come to him*. He is within my reach, only a prayer away. Faith means that I commit my past, present and future to him, knowing that if I do so, it will be well with my soul.

Faith alone in Christ alone—that's the message of the Bible's story.

Only one guarantee

By trusting in this Jesus we can have the absolute and ultimate assurance: 'Believe in the Lord Jesus, *and you will be saved.*' This is a matter of truth and trust, a matter of taking Jesus at his word.

Will you do that today? Only then can you be absolutely sure that God has dealt with your past, and that he has a purpose for your future, and that he will guide your present.

And if you do, three things will be vital for your life as a Christian:

Read, read, read, your Bible! You will never tire of the story. You will find that it is constantly up to date, relevant and practical. You will discover depths to it that will stretch your mind, visions that will warm your heart, and precepts that will shape your destiny. Live by it; it is still true that 'Man shall not live by bread alone, but by every word that comes from the mouth of God' (Matthew 4:4).

Find a Bible-believing and gospel-preaching church. Jesus saves us individually, but only so that he can make us part of his family. His family is the church, and we are the church when we meet together in Christ's name week by week to worship the living God. Be part of the church!

Grow in your knowledge of the Christian faith. There are many resources available for deepening your understanding of the Bible story. There are good books available which will enrich and instruct you. There are Internet resources which you can download. Live life to the full! Live as a Christian! Let the joy of Jesus Christ be in you, through the words of his truth and the doctrines of his Word!

And remember, the gospel story of the Bible urges us to remember the single most important issue of life:

Whoever believes in the Son has eternal life; whoever does not obey the Son shall not see life, but the wrath of God remains on him (John 3:36).

On the first day of the week
God, the Christian and the Sabbath

IAIN D CAMPBELL

ISBN 978–1–903087–95–4

240PP PAPERBACK

In an increasingly secular world, the personal and social benefits of Sabbath-keeping are being lost to us more and more. It is increasingly difficult to defend the traditional view that the fourth commandment is still binding on us, and that God wants us to honour the first day of the week, the Lord's Day, as a Christian Sabbath. This book examines some of the issues raised in this debate, and argues that for the Christian believer, the Sabbath principle is one which is still binding, relevant, necessary and beneficial.

This book examines some of the issues raised in the Sabbath debate, and argues that for the Christian believer, the Sabbath principle is one which is still binding, relevant, necessary and beneficial.

'Dr Campbell's book is a joy to read. It is well written and easy to understand.'
JOEL BEEKE

IAIN D CAMPBELL

ISBN 978–1–84625–029–3

160PP PAPERBACK

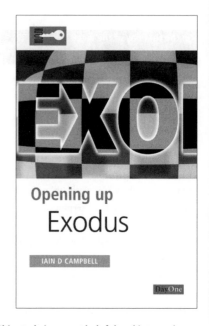

Opening up
Exodus

IAIN D CAMPBELL

DayOne

By the time we have read through Exodus, we have learned the basic vocabulary of the gospel— words like blood, redeem, sacrifice, glory, law, tabernacle, passover are all here, part of the great drama in which God saves a people for himself. To study Exodus, therefore, is to come to the heart of the message of redemption, to see God as the Saviour of his people, caring for them and present with them as they journey from Egypt to Canaan, from the house of bondage to the land of promise. Join the journey now.

This series of books, which open up the Bible, include the following features:

- Priced to suit the pocket
- Excellent introduction to the background and text of each Bible book
- Map and timeline included in each book
- 'For further study' and 'To think about and discuss' questions
- Ideal for small groups and family devotions
- Application of the message of the Bible to modern situations

'This study is a most helpful and interesting introduction to the Book of Exodus … It also contains the rarest of features: excellent discussion questions. I recommend it highly.'
W Robert Godfrey, Professor of Church History and President of Westminster Seminary, California

The Gospel according to Ruth
Devotional studies in the book of Ruth

IAIN D CAMPBELL

ISBN 978–1–903087–36–7

128PP PAPERBACK

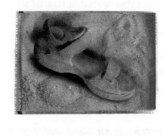

Ruth, by grace, was brought from Moab into the covenant community of God's people, and consequently into the line from which Christ came. The author sees this as an example of the same grace by which we can become partakers of the blessings of God's salvation through the work of the great Redeemer, the Lord Jesus Christ.

'These studies present the story of Ruth as, effectively, 'the Old Testament in miniature'. The great themes of sin and grace, of covenant blessing and chastisement, of God's welcome of Gentile 'strangers and foreigners' into his own covenant community and the coming of a Son (Ruth's and David's) as Redeemer, are all skilfully handled from the narrative in an eye-opening and heart-warming manner.'

From a review in *The Stornoway Gazette*

'Iain Campbell demonstrates in a masterful way that the story of Ruth is the Old Testament in a miniature. Another useful commentary that should be found in our bookcase—after it has been thoroughly enjoyed.'

GRAPEVINE

About Day One:

Day One's threefold commitment:

- To be faithful to the Bible, God's inerrant, infallible Word;
- To be relevant to our modern generation;
- To be excellent in our publication standards.

I continue to be thankful for the publications of Day One. They are biblical; they have sound theology; and they are relative to the issues at hand. The material is condensed and manageable while, at the same time, being complete—a challenging balance to find. We are happy in our ministry to make use of these excellent publications.

JOHN MACARTHUR, PASTOR-TEACHER, GRACE COMMUNITY CHURCH, CALIFORNIA

It a great encouragement to see Day One making such excellent progress. Their publications are always biblical, accessible and attractively produced, with no compromise on quality. Long may their progress continue and increase!

JOHN BLANCHARD, AUTHOR, EVANGELIST AND APOLOGIST

Visit our website for more information and to request a free catalogue of our books.

www.dayone.co.uk